A PICTORIAL ENCYCLOPEDIA OF
THE ORIENTAL ARTS

A PICTORIAL ENCYCLOPEDIA OF
THE ORIENTAL ARTS

edited by KADOKAWA SHOTEN

CROWN PUBLISHERS, INC. NEW YORK

A PICTORIAL ENCYCLOPEDIA OF THE ORIENTAL ARTS, compiled from the
Oriental section of the ENCYCLOPEDIA OF WORLD ART published by
Kadokawa Shoten Publishing Company, Tokyo, 1968, is published in
the United States of America, 1969 by Crown Publishers, Inc.,
419 Park Avenue South, New York, N. Y. 10016

Published simultaneously in Canada by General Publishing Company
Limited

The following scholars shared the editing as indicated
below:
       KOREA by Mikami Tsugio

Printed in Japan .

Table of Contents

LIST OF PLATES

Korea

COLOR PLATES

1. Bronze tube with gold and silver inlay. Excavated from a tomb at Pyongyang. $10^1/_4$ in. in length, $1^3/_4$ in. in diameter. Lolang Period.
2. Buckle. Excavated from a tomb at Pyongyang. Silver. $5 \times 2^1/_2$ in. Lolang Period. National Museum of Korea, Seoul.
3. Box painted with colored lacquer (side view). Excavated from Chaehyob Tomb at Pyongyang. Bamboo. $15^1/_3$ in. in length, 7 in. in width. Lolang Period. Historical Museum of Korea, Pyongyang.
4. Desk painted with colored lacquer (top surface). Excavated from Chaehyob Tomb at Pyongyang. Wood. $30^1/_2$ in. in length, $21^1/_4$ in. in width. Lolang Period. National Museum of Korea, Seoul.
5. Lacquered tray. Excavated from Wang Kwang Tomb at Pyongyang. About $10^2/_3$ in. in diameter. Lolang Period. National Museum of Korea, Seoul.
6. Gilt bronze openwork fitting. Excavated from Tomb No. 1, Chinpa-ri. Chunghwa-kun, Pyongan-numdo. Koguryo Dynasty. 6th century. Historical Museum of Korea, Pyongyang.
7. Hsüan-wu (snake-tortoise). Wall painting in Great Tomb of Woohyon-ri, Summo-ri, Kangso-kun, Pyongan-numdo. Koguryo Dynasty. Second half of 6th–first half of 7th century.
8. Ts'ang-lung (dragon). Wall painting in Great Tomb of Woohyon-ri, Summo-ri, Kangso-kun, Pyngan-numdo. Koguryo Dynasty. Second half of 6th–first half of 7th century.
9. Wrestling scene. Wall painting in Kakcho Tomb (wrestlers), Chian, Chilin-shêng, China. Koguryo Dynasty. Second half of 5th–first half of 6th century.
10. Chu-chüeh (phoenix). Wall painting in Middle Tomb of Woohyon-ri, Summo-ri, Kangso-kun, Pyongan-numdo. Koguryo Dynasty. Second half of 6th–first half of 7th century.
11. Master of a house. Wall painting in Tomb No. 3, Anak, Anak-kun, Hwanghae-numdo. Koguryo Dynasty. Second half of 4th century.
12. Housewife. Wall painting in Tomb No. 3, Anak, Anak-kun, Hwanghae-numdo. Koguryo Dynasty. Second half of 4th century.
13. Procession scene. Wall painting in Tomb No. 3, Anak, Anak-kun, Hwanghae-numdo. Koguryo Dynasty. Second half of 4th century.
14. Hunting scene. Wall painting in Mu-yong Tomb (Tomb of dancers), Chian, Chilin-shêng, China. Koguryo Dynasty. Second half of 5th–first half of 6th century.
15. Incense burner with long handle. Excavated from Koomkwan Tomb, Kyongsang-pukdo. Bronze. Old Silla (Three Kingdoms period) Dynasty. Kyongju Branch, National Museum of Korea, Kyongju.
16. Wall painting in a tomb (copy). Noongsan-ri, Puyo-kun, Chungchong-numdo. Paekche Dynasty.
17. Bodhisattva in meditative pose. Gilt bronze. $32^1/_2$ in. in height. Paekche Dynasty. National Museum of Korea, Seoul.
18. Bodhisattva in meditative pose (detail). Gilt bronze. $32^3/_4$ in. in height. Paekche Dynasty. Toksu Palace Museum, Seoul.
19. Gold crown. Excavated from Sobong Tomb, Kyongsang-pukdo. About $13^3/_4$ in. in height. Old Silla (Three Kingdoms period) Dynasty. National Museum of Korea, Seoul.
20. Tile with image of one of Four Heavenly Kings. Excavated from the ruins of Green wang-sa Temple, Kyongsang-pukdo. Yellow-green glaze. Great Silla Dynasty. National Museum of Korea, Seoul.

21. Stone pagoda of Punhwan-sa Temple. 634 A.D. Suburbs of Kyongju, Kyongsang-pukdo.
22. Pulkuksa Temple. Great Silla Dynasty. Chin-hyon-ri, Kyongju, Kyongsang-pukdo.
23. Cinerary urn. Excavated from suburbs of Kyonju. About 19 in. in height. Yellow glaze. Great Silla Dynasty. National Museum of Korea, Seoul.
24. Covered circular box with arabesque design in mother-of-pearl inlay. 5 in. in diameter, $1^3/_4$ in. in height. Koryo Dynasty. Taima-ji Temple, Nara, Japan.
25. Incense burner with arabesque design in silver inlay. Koryo Dynasty. Historical Museum of Korea, Pyongyang.
26. Ewer and stand, with openwork design of lotus scrolls. Celadon. Koryo Dynasty. National Museum of Korea, Seoul.
27. Box with openwork design of peony scrolls. Celadon. $4^2/_3$ in. in height, 9 in. in mouth diameter. Koryo Dynasty. National Museum, Tokyo.
28. Gourd-shaped ewer with lotus-petal design. Celadon with underglaze red. About $11^3/_4$ in. in height. Koryo Dynasty.
29. Ewer with engraved lotus-scroll design. Celadon. $14^2/_3$ in. in height. Koryo Dynasty. Nezu Art Museum, Tokyo. (Important cultural property.)
30. Avalokiteśvara with willow branch (detail). By Hye Ho. 56 in. in height. Koguryo Dynasty. Sensō-ji Temple, Tokyo.
31. Portrait of a king of Korea. Color on silk. $52^1/_4 \times 29$ in. Yi Dynasty. Sōan-ji Temple, Hikone, Japan.
32. Flask, "Engraved Mishima" type (patterns embossed). Ceramics. $9^1/_4$ in. in height, $6^1/_3$ in. in width. Yi Dynasty.
33. Vase with lotus and willow design, "Mishima" type (with strawrope patterns resembling the letters of the calendar published by Mishima-jinja Shrine, Shizuoka, Japan). Ceramics. 13 in. in height, $6^1/_3$ in. in width. Early Yi Dynasty.
34. Water dropper with figure design, blue and white, underglaze coppered. Ceramics. $2^1/_2$ in. in height, 3 in. in width. Yi Dynasty.
35. Beveled jar, underglaze coppered. Ceramics. 8 in. in height, $8^3/_4$ in. in width. Yi Dynasty.
36. Jar with plum-blossom design, blue and white. Ceramics. $16^2/_3$ in. in height, $12^3/_4$ in. in width. Yi Dynasty. Japan Folk Craft Museum, Tokyo.
37. Smoking-set box with silver inlay. Iron. $2^1/_4$ in. in height, 4 in. in diameter. Yi Dynasty. Japan Folk Craft Museum, Tokyo.
38. Box covered with sliced horn. $9^1/_2 \times 13^1/_3 \times 6$ in. Yi Dynasty. National Museum, Tokyo.

GRAVURE PLATES

1. Earthenware with comb-mark patterns. Excavated from Yomdo-ri, Yongung-kun, Pyongan-numdo. $10^2/_3$ in. in height, $7^1/_3$ in. in maximum diameter. Stone Age. Kyoto University, Kyoto.
2. Jar with painted ornament. Excavated near Lake Yongsu, Woonggi-kun, Hamgyongpukdo. $7^3/_4$ in. in height. Stone Age.
3. Spouted vessel. Excavated from Yongson-don, Pusan. About $6^1/_3$ in. in maximum diameter. Stone Age.
4. Earthenware with comb-mark patterns. Excavated from Yongson-don, Pusan. $5^1/_2$ in. in height, 6 in. in maximum diameter. Stone Age.
5. Roof tiles. Excavated from Pyongyang. Lolang Period. Tokyo University, Tokyo.
6. Shoulder piece, with hunting-scene design. Excavated near Kyongju. Bronze. About $11^3/_4$ in. in length. Calcolithic Age.
7. *Ting* (tripod). Earthenware. Excavated from Pyongyang. $12^3/_4$ in. in height. Lolang Period. Tokyo University, Tokyo.
8. Clay seals. Excavated from Pyongyang. Lolang Period. Tokyo University, Tokyo.
9. *Tou* (stem bowl). Earthenware. Excavated from Pyongyang. $4^2/_3$ in. in height. Lolang Period. Tokyo University, Tokyo.
10. Guard of Spear. Excavated from Sokam-ri, Pyongyang. Iron. Lolang Period. National Museum of Korea, Seoul.

11. Horse. Excavated from Chaehyob (painted basket) Tomb at Pyongyang. Wood. 23²/₃ in. in height. Lolang Period. National Museum of Korea, Seoul.

12. Incense burner with hill-shaped cover. Excavated from a tomb at Pyongyang. Bronze. 8 in. in height. Lolang Period. National Museum of Korea, Seoul.

13. Jade Pi (ritual disk). Excavated from tomb at Pyongyang. 8¹/₃ in. in diameter. Lolang Period. National Museum of Korea, Seoul.

14. Bronze mirror with design of figure subjects and inscription "Shang Fang." Excavated from a tomb at Pyongyang. Lolang Period. National Museum of Korea, Seoul.

15. Shogun-zuka (General's tomb). Chian, Chilin-shêng, China. Koguryo Dynasty (second half of 5th century).

16. Procession scene. Wall painting in Tomb No. 12, Chian, Chilin shêng, China. Koguryo Dynasty (second half of 5th–first half of 6th century).

17. Kitchen scene. Wall painting in Tomb No. 3, Anak, Anak-kun, Hwanghae-numdo. Koguryo Dynasty (second half of 4th century).

18. Procession scene. Wall painting in Tomb No. 3, Anak-kun, Hwanghae-numdo. Koguryo Dynasty (second half of 4th century).

19. Arabesque wall painting in Sashin Tomb (Tomb of the four spirits), Chian, Chilin-shêng, China. Koguryo Dynasty (second half of 6th–early 7th century).

20. Taoistic immortal. Wall painting in Sashin Tomb (Tomb of the four spirits), Chian, Chilin-shêng, China. Koguryo Dynasty (second half of 6th–early 7th century).

21. *Hsüan-wu* (snake-tortoise). Wall painting in Sashin Tomb (Tomb of the four spirits) Chian, Chilin-shêng. Koguryo Dynasty (second half of 6th–early 7th century).

22. Gilt-bronze openwork fitting (detail). Excavated from Tomb No. 1, Chinpa-ri, Chunghwa-kun, Pyongyan-numdo. Koguryo Dynasty (6th century). Historical Museum of Korea, Pyongyang.

23. Epitaph for King Hong Thae. Chian, Chilin-shêng, China. Koguryo Dynasty (early 5th century).

24. Monumental inscription. Mu Du Ru Tomb, Chian, Chilin-shêng, China. Koguryo Dynasty (second half of 5th–first half of 6th century).

25. Tile with phoenix design. Excavated from Kyuam-myon, Puyo-kun, Chungchong-numdo. About 16¹/₄ in. square. Paekche Dynasty. National Museum of Korea, Seoul.

26. Tile with arabesque design. Excavated from Kyuam-myon, Puyo-kun, Chungchong-numdo. About 16¹/₄ in. square. Paekche Dynasty. National Museum of Korea, Seoul.

27. Tile with goblin figure. Excavated from Kyuam-myon, Puyo-kun, Chungchong-numdo. About 16¹/₄ in. square. Paekche Dynasty. National Museum of Korea, Seoul.

28. Tile with landscape design. Excavated from Kyuam-myon, Puyo-kun, Chungchong-numdo. About 16¹/₄ in. square. Paekche Dynasty. National Museum of Korea, Seoul.

29. Tile burial chamber and wall painting. Sonsun-ri, Kongju-kun, Chungchong-numdo. Paekche Dynasty.

30. Boat-shaped vessel. Excavated from Kumnyong (golden bell) Tomb, Kyongsang-pukdo. About 5 in. in height. Old Silla Dynasty.

31. Bodhisattva. Excavated from Kunsoo-ri, Puyo-kun, Chungchong-numdo. Gilt Bronze. 8¹/₃ in. in height. Paekche Dynasty. National Museum of Korea, Seoul.

32. Buddha. Excavated from Kunsoo-ri, Puyo-kun, Chungchong-numdo. Alabaster. 4¹/₂ in. in height. Paekche Dynasty. National Museum of Korea, Seoul.

33. Buddha and two attendants. Relief on rock cliff, Yonghyon-ri, Sosun-kun, Chungchong-numdo. Paekche Dynasty.

34. Jar. Excavated near Kyongju, Kyongsang-pukdo. Old Silla Dynasty.

35. Covered jar with handle. Excavated from near Kyongju, Kyongsang-pukdo. Old Silla Dynasty.

36. Bowl with tall foot. Excavated near Kyongju, Kyongsang-pukdo. Old Silla Dynasty.

37. Earrings with gold filigree. Excavated from a tomb at Kyongju, Kyongsang-pukdo. About 3¹/₄ in. in over-all length. Old Silla Dynasty. National Museum of Korea, Seoul.

38. Head of Buddha. Excavated from ruins of a temple near Kyongju, Kyongsang-pukdo. 3¹/₄ in. in height. Old Silla Dynasty. Kyongju Branch, National Museum of Korea, Kyongju.

39. Bodhisattva in meditative pose. Excavated from Sowak-ri, Kyongju. Granite. Old Silla Dynasty. Kyongju Branch, National Museum of Korea, Kyongju.

40. Bell for King Sondok. 131 in. in height, 89¹/₃ in. in maximum diameter. Great Silla Dynasty. Kyongju Branch, National Museum of Korea, Kyongju.
41. Stele at the Tomb of King Thae Chog (Mu Yol). 661 A.D. Punae-myon, Kyongsan-pukdo.
42. Bhaisajyaguru. Gilt bronze. 12³/₄ in. in height. Great Silla Dynasty. Museum of Fine Arts, Boston.
43. Vairocana. Gilt bronze. 67³/₄ in. in height. Middle of 8th century. Buddha Hall of Pulkuk-sa Temple, Chinyon-ri, Kyongju-kun, Kyongsang-pukdo.
44. Amitābha (detail). Gold. Discovered in the stone three-storied pagoda on the ruins of Hwangbok-sa Temple. 7 in. in height. Early 8th century.
45. Sakyamuni (detail). Granite. 134²/₃ in. in height. Middle of 8th century. Sokkulam Temple, Kyongju, Kyongsang-pukdo.
46. Three-storied pagoda, Shilsang-sa Temple. About 311 in. in height. Middle of 9th century. Ibbsok-ri, Sunae-myon, Jolla-pukdo.
47. Pagoda, Pulkuk-sa Temple. 409¹/₂ in. in height. Middle of 8th century. Chinhyon-ri, Kyongju-kun, Kyongsang-pukdo.
48. Five-storied pagoda in Hwaohm-sa Temple. End of 9th century. Hwangjon-ri, Masun-myon, Jolla-numdo.
49. Stone pagoda of four lions in Hwaohm-sa Temple. End of 9th century. Hwangjon-ri, Masun-myon, Jolla-numdo.
50. Stone figures of monkey (above) and ram (below). Tomb of a king. Kyongju, Oedoong-myon, Kyongsang-pukdo. Great Silla Dynasty.
51. Stone figure of man. Tomb of a king. Kyongju, Oedoong-myon, Kyongsang-pukdo. Great Silla Dynasty.
52. Vajradhara engraved on stone door. Attributed to a tomb at Soak-ri, Kyongju, Kyongsang-pukdo. 59³/₄ × 18 in. Great Silla Dynasty. Toksu Palace Museum, Seoul.
53. Goblin-mask handles. Attributed to a tomb at Soak-ri, Kyongju, Kyongsang-pukdo. Bronze. 6¹/₂ in. in over-all length. Great Silla Dynasty. National Museum of Korea, Seoul.
54. Roof tiles. Phoenix, man-birds and Hōsōge (imaginary) flower. Great Silla Dynasty.
55. Roof tiles. Heavenly beings, arabesque, birds with flowers in the bills and phoenixes. Great Silla Dynasty.
56. Roof tile with lotus-flower design. Excavated from the ruins of Imhae Palace. Kyongju. Great Silla Dynasty.
57. Roof tile with giraffe design. Great Silla Dynasty.
58. Roof tile with moon design. Excavated from Kyongju. 5¹/₂ in. in diameter. Great Silla Dynasty. National Museum of Korea, Seoul.
59. Gargoyle. Excavated from ruins of temple, Kyongju. Great Silla Dynasty.
60. Tile with Hōsōge (imaginary) flower design. Excavated from ruins of Imhae Palace, Kyongju. 12²/₃ in. square. Great Silla Dynasty.
61. Roof tile with hunting-scene design. Excavated from Sajong-ri, Kyongju. 6 in. in length. Great Silla Dynasty. National Museum of Korea, Seoul.
62. Sarira casket of Kamun-sa Temple. Excavated from Youngbok-myon, Kyongsang-pukdo. Great Silla Dynasty. National Museum of Korea, Seoul.
63. Cinerary urn with stamped ornament. Excavated from Kyongju, Kyongsang-pukdo. 14 in. in over-all height. Great Silla Dynasty.
64. Head of Buddha. Bronze. Early Koryo Dynasty.
65. Sakyamuni. Iron. Late Silla–early Koryo Dynasty. Koonjyong Palace at Kyongbok Palace, Seoul.
66. Amitābha. Stucco. 106 in. in height. Koryo Dynasty. Pusok-sa Temple, Pusok-myon, Kyongsang-pukdo.
67. Maitreya. Stone. About 669¹/₃ in. in height. Early Koryo Dynasty. Kwangchok-sa Temple, Chungcnong-numdo.
68. Mask of court servant. Wood. Late Koryo Dynasty. National Museum of Korea, Seoul.
69. Bhaisajyaguru. Relief on rock cliff, Yaksakok, Kwangju-kun, Kyonggwi-do. 977 A.D.
70. Memorial pagoda for Priest Chi Kwang of Pobchon-sa Temple (upper part). 1085 A.D. Kyongbok Palace, Seoul.
71. Stone octagonal nine-storied pagoda. About 472¹/₂ in. in height. Koryo Dynasty. Wolchong-sa Temple, Chinpu-myon, Kangwon-do.

72. Buddha Hall of Soodook-sa Temple (detail). Dooksun-myon, Chungchong-numdo. 1308 A.D.
73. Lobed vase. Celadon. Koryo Dynasty. Cleveland Museum of Art, Cleveland.
74. Ewer with lotus-petal design in relief. Celadon. Koryo Dynasty. Brooklyn Museum, New York.
75. Ewer with engraved lotus-scroll design. Celadon. Koryo Dynasty. Nezu Art Museum, Tokyo.
76. Square incense burner with relief ornament. Celadon. 7 in. in maximun diameter. Koryo Dynasty.
77. Figure of monkey with its baby. Celadon. $4^{1}/_{4}$ in. in height. Koryo Dynasty.
78. Figure of duck. Celadon. $3^{3}/_{4}$ in. in height. Koryo Dynasty.
79. Pillow with lion supports. Inlaid celadon. $4^{2}/_{3}$ in. in height. Koryo Dynasty. Toksu Palace Museum, Seoul.
80. Sherd with openwork design of interlocking circles. Celadon. Koryo Dynasty. Cleveland Museum of Art, Cleveland.
81. Gourd-shaped ewer and stand with child design. Inlaid celadon with copper-red underglaze. About $11^{3}/_{4}$ in. in height. Koryo Dynasty. Toksu Palace Museum, Seoul.
82. Ewer with bamboo design. Celadon with underglaze brown-black. Koryo Dynasty. Art Institute of Chicago, Chicago.
83. Vase with reed and heron design. Inlaid celadon. $13^{1}/_{4}$ in. in height. Koryo Dynasty. National Museum, Tokyo.
84. Jar with "Seven Luminaries" design in brown-black. Celadon. $3^{1}/_{2}$ in. in height. Koryo Dynasty.
85. Vase with flowering plant design within reserve panels. White ware. $11^{1}/_{3}$ in. in height. Koryo Dynasty. Toksu Palace Museum, Seoul.
86. Vase with Ginseng-leaf design in white. Black ware. $11^{1}/_{2}$ in. in height. Koryo Dynasty.
87. Apsara on a temple bell. Koryo Dynasty. Nagato-ichinomiya-jinja Shrine, Yamaguchi, Japan.
88. Amulet cases. Silver. $2^{1}/_{2}$ in. in diameter, $5^{2}/_{3}$ in. in height. Koryo Dynasty.
89. Box with arabesque design in mother-of-pearl inlay. $14^{3}/_{4} \times 7^{1}/_{2} \times 11^{3}/_{4}$ in. Koryo Dynasty. National Museum, Tokyo.
90. Mirror with sea-animal design. Bronze. 7 in. in diameter. Koryo Dynasty.
91. Covered box with arabesque design in mother-of-pearl inlay. $3^{2}/_{3}$ in. in maximum diameter, $1^{1}/_{3}$ in. in height. Koryo Dynasty. Keishun-in Temple, Kyoto.
92. Ewer with inlaid willow and water-bird design. $14^{3}/_{4}$ in. in height. Koryo Dynasty. National Museum of Korea, Seoul.
93. Visit in dream to T'ao-yüan (detail). By An Kyon. Ink and faint color on silk. Yi Dynasty. Tenri Library, Tenri, Japan.
94. Landscape and flower-and-bird (detail). Two of four-fold screen. Ink on paper. Yi Dynasty. Seiken-ji Temple, Shizuoka, Japan.
95. Landscapes (detail). Eight-fold screen. Ink on paper. $38^{2}/_{3} \times$ about $157^{1}/_{2}$ in. Yi Dynasty. Daigan-ji Temple, Hiroshima, Japan.
96. Grapevine. Ink on paper. 40×13 in. Yi Dynasty.
97. Grapevine. Ink on paper. $45 \times 16^{1}/_{2}$ in. Yi Dynasty.
98. Grapevine and squirrels. Ink on paper. $37^{3}/_{4} \times 12^{1}/_{4}$ in. Yi Dynasty.
99. Myna bird on pine branch. Ink on paper. $17^{1}/_{3} \times 8^{2}/_{3}$ in. Yi Dynasty.
100. Wildgeese and reeds. Ink on silk. $51^{1}/_{2} \times 13^{2}/_{3}$ in. Yi Dynasty.
101. Bamboo and rocks. Ink on silk. $47^{1}/_{2} \times 13^{3}/_{4}$ in. Yi Dynasty.
102. Autumn landscape. Ink on silk. $47^{1}/_{2} \times 14$ in. Yi Dynasty.
103. Palsung-jon of Pobju-sa Temple. Wood. Poun-kun, Chungchong-pukdo. Yi Dynasty.
104. Taeson-jon of Mun-myo (Confucian temple). Wood. Yi Dynasty. Seoul.
105. Kunjong-jon of Kyongbok Palace (interior). Wood. Yi Dynasty. Seoul.
106. Flask with arabesque design. "Mishima" type (with strawrope patterns resembling the letters of the calendar published by Mishima-jinja Shrine, Shizuoka, Japan). Excavated from Cheju Island. Ceramics. 8 in. in height, $6^{3}/_{4}-5^{2}/_{3}$ in. in diameter. Yi Dynasty.
107. Jar with fish and bird design painted over brush-mark slip. Ceramics. $12^{3}/_{4}$ in. in height, $9^{1}/_{4}$ in. in width. Yi Dynasty.
108 Ceramic teabowl, "Mishima" type, incised decoration. $4^{1}/_{4}$ in. in height, $5^{1}/_{4}$ in. in diameter.

Yi Dynasty.

109. Ceramic bowl with brush-mark slip and scratch design. $7^1/_2$ in. in maximum diameter. Yi Dynasty. Japan Folk Craft Museum, Tokyo.
110. Ceramic teabowl with brush-mark slip. "Mishima" type. $2^1/_2$ in. in height, $6^3/_4$ in. in maximum diameter. Yi Dynasty. Japan Folk Craft Museum, Tokyo.
111. Jar with grapevine design, underglaze of blue and black-brown painting. Ceramics. $13^1/_2$ in. in height, $10^3/_4$ in. in width. Yi Dynasty. Japan Folk Craft Museum, Tokyo.
112. Tea bowl with black-brown inlay decoration. Ceramics. 3 in. in height, $6^1/_3$ in. in diameter. Yi Dynasty. Japan Folk Craft Museum, Tokyo.
113. Jar with heron design, underglaze black-brown. Ceramics. 12 in. in height, 12 in. in diameter. Yi Dynasty.
114. Jar with grass design, underglaze black-brown. Ceramics. $8^1/_3$ in. in height, $7^1/_2$ in. in width. Yi Dynasty.
115. Jar with dragon design, underglaze black-brown. Ceramics. 10 in. in height, $10^1/_2$ in. in width. Yi Dynasty.
116. Bowl with water-fowl design, blue and white. Ceramics. 5 in. in height, 15 in. in diameter. Yi Dynasty. Japan Folk Craft Museum, Tokyo.
117. Square vase with roundel design, blue and white. Ceramics. $9^1/_4$ in. in height, $4^1/_4$ in. in width. Yi Dynasty.
118. Flask with pink-flower design, blue and white. Ceramics. $7^1/_2$ in. in height, 7 in. in width. Yi Dynasty.
119. Ribbed jar. White porcelain. $7^2/_3$ in. in height, $6^1/_2$ in. in width. Yi Dynasty.
120. Vase, red underglaze. Ceramics. 7 in. in height, $4^1/_4$ in. in diameter. Yi Dynasty.
121. Octagonal bottle, white porcelain. $7^1/_4$ in. in height, $5^1/_4$ in. in width. Yi Dynasty.
122. Water dropper in shape of frog. White porcelain. 2 in. in height, $3^1/_3$ in. in width. Yi Dynasty.
123. Water dropper in shape of plum blossom, blue glaze. Ceramics. $1^1/_3$ in. in height, 3 in. in width. Yi Dynasty.
124. Water dropper in shape of house, blue and white. Ceramics. $1^2/_3$ in. in height, $2^1/_4$ in. in width. Yi Dynasty. Japan Folk Craft Museum, Tokyo.
125. Water dropper with plum-blossom design, blue and white. 3 in. in height, $2^2/_3$ in width. Yi Dynasty.
126. Writing box with flower-and-bird design in mother-of-pearl inlay. $9^1/_3 \times 8^2/_3$ in. Yi Dynasty. National Museum, Tokyo.
127. Box with floral patterns in mother-of-pearl inlay. $18 \times 13^3/_4 \times 5^1/_2$ in. Yi Dynasty.
128. Box with grapevine and squirrel design in mother-of-pearl inlay. Yi Dynasty.
129. Seal box. Wood. 6 in. in height, 9 in. in length. Yi Dynasty. Japan Folk Craft Museum, Tokyo.

KOREA

Relations Between Korea and Japan

The geographical location of Korea, a large peninsula of the Asian continent, suggests the role she played in the cultural history of the Far East. The Japanese Islands form an arc off the coast of the Asian continent and resemble a baby suckling at its mother's breast: the nursing mother is Korea. The islands between the two countries can be likened to drops of milk. This simile, of course, implies a very close relationship, with nourishment flowing outward from the mother to her infant. And, indeed, Japan was nourished by Continental culture in just such a way. The channel separating Korea and Japan is only 120 miles wide, and this proximity permitted an easy flow of new techniques and ideas from Asia into Japan.

While Japan was still in the Stone Age, a highly developed bronze culture existed in China and northern Asia. The bronze culture of China, at its peak during the Chou Dynasty, spread to southern Manchuria and along the coasts of Korea down through the peninsula, then to Japan. Thus, since very ancient times, Korea has been an intermediary for the passage of Asian culture, especially Chinese, into Japan.

The difference between the levels of cultural development in China and that in Japan was always so great that a mediator was necessary. Manchuria and Korea both served this function, saving Japan from being inundated with new ideas and giving her time to absorb things more naturally. For example, Japan learned of Buddhism and Confucianism from Korea, where these two teachings from China had been already assimilated. Korea played this role of cultural mediator not only in ancient times but also in the middle and modern ages. Of course, the flow was not always one way; at times, Japan sent expeditionary forces toward the Asian continent. Thus Korea developed a peculiar culture formed under influences from Japan as well as from China and northern Asia.

In this regard, neither the study of Japan nor of Korea can be complete without considering the historical relationship between the two countries. From the third or fourth century A. D. to the sixth century, Japan's centralized government ruled a part of South Korea and made it an important base of economic expansion. In terms of culture, however, Japan was influenced by Korea. It is no wonder, therefore, that to some extent the two countries yielded similar cultural products. For instance, the weapons found in the ancient tomb mounds of the period known as the Three Kingdoms in Korea and those found in ancient Japanese tombs show conspicuous similarity; the tombs themselves resemble each other closely. One can also note that the use of comma-shaped jewels, *magatama*, was almost exclusively limited to southern Korea and Japan.

In addition to the introduction of Buddhism, Chinese characters, and other learning, the important roles played by Koreans who emigrated to Japan at one time or another should also be remembered. During the Silla period (668–935), the intimate relationship between Japan and Silla was occasionally interrupted by political upheavals in this part of Asia, but, nevertheless, many merchants and Buddhist priests emigrated to Japan, thus maintaining almost continuous economic and cultural ties. Pao-Kao Chang, a wealthy merchant of Silla, was among the most well-known of these travelers. The Japanese authorities permitted commercial transactions with such merchants as Chang because many Japanese nobles were anxious to purchase Chinese cultural products from them. In those times, there was scarcely any possibility of direct intercourse between China and Japan.

During the Koryo period (935–1392), two unfortunate events occurred which affected relations between the two countries. One was the Mongol invasion of Japan, for which Korea was forced to serve as a military base. The real aggressors in this invasion were, however, the Mongols; the people of Korea suffered as much at their hands as did the Japanese. Indeed, the coercion was so severe that a resistance movement of Korean people against their conquerors grew. The other event was the invasion of Korea by Japanese pirates, so-called *wakō*. Taking advantage of the loose controls placed on maritime activity by Japan's Muromachi government, these pirates infested the southern coasts of Korea. They inflicted such great damage that this was counted as one of the main reasons for the fall of the Koryo Dynasty. Such pirates, however, were mainly dismissed warriors or profiteers; their criminal deeds were of a private nature, not perpetrated on a national scale.

These were exceptional events, and the two countries usually maintained close, friendly relations. Many merchants and Buddhist priests continued to travel back and forth. Japan sent official vessels, called *Kangōsen*, to purchase Chinese products, and Korea built a special inn at Kumhae to receive her Japanese guests. Although Japanese visited primarily to acquire Chinese cultural products through the hands of the Koreans, they also brought back to Japan Korean Buddhist articles and many famous Korean celadons. The beautiful lacquered incense box preserved at Taimai-ji Temple is a typical example of Buddhist art. Thus, the two countries enjoyed a generally friendly relationship, although infrequent crises did occur. The attack of the Toi pirates on northern Kyūshū at the beginning of the eleventh century was another of these unfortunate episodes.

During the Yi Dynasty, which was established toward the end of the fourteenth century, relations between Korea and Japan were peaceful. In the first half of the Yi period, the government permitted trade with Japan, and trade with the feudal lords in the western parts of Japan was particulary prosperous. The government designated three trade ports, and large numbers of Japanese settled in their vicinity. At one point, Japanese settlers rioted against the severe controls of the Yi Dynasty, but it was just a temporary disturbance.

The latter half of the Yi period corresponds to the Edo period in Japan. Trade was continuous, although not so prosperous as it had been earlier. The two governments exchanged diplomatic and other types of envoys. A monopoly on Japanese trade activity with Korea was given to the feudal lords of Tsushima (the Sō family), who were instrumental in the exchange of products and culture between the two nations. By the terms of this monopoly agreement, Japan could continually be in contact with the Korean Peninsula and thus had every opportunity to import both Chinese and Korean products. In the middle of the Yi period, however, the Japanese, under the direction of Toyotomi Hideyoshi, invaded Korea (1592). He intended to use Korea as a base from which to attack China, but of course inflicted great damage on Korea and left the Korean people with the regrettable impression that the Japanese were aggressive invaders.

Still, as previously mentioned, the relationship between Korea and Japan remained generally good and hostilities were few and infrequent until the nineteenth century. This amicable connection is conspicuously different from the pattern of Korea's relations with countries of the Asian continent. One undesirable result of the introduction of modern capitalism was that relations between the two countries worsened toward the end of the nineteenth century. A modern trade treaty was signed between Korea and Japan in 1876, but Korea was slower than Japan in adapting herself to the Western world. This created many problems. Two revolts, one in 1882 and the other in 1884, were followed by severe political complications. In addition to Korea's domestic problems, caused by a growing antagonism between conservative and progressive factions within the government, China, Japan, and Russia were all fighting for control of Korea. These conflicts finally resulted in the Russo-Japanese War (1904–1905). Despite vigorous opposition by the Korean people, Japan gradually took over the country and annexed it in 1910. The Japanese ruled there until their surrender at the end of World War II, when the United States and the Soviet Union arranged to divide the country at the now-famous thirty-eighth parallel. Even today, political tensions caused by this division are far from being satisfactorily resolved.

Korea's Role in the History of the Far East

The foregoing explanation is not comprehensive enough to clarify the parts that Manchuria and Korea played in northeast Asian history. They had several other important roles besides that of cultural bridges to Japan.

The area around thirty degrees north parallel contains the boundary between Korea and Manchuria, the Liaotung Peninsula, and the starting point of the Great Wall of China, which runs from Kuan on the coast of Pohai Bay thousands of miles westward. The Great Wall was built by the Ch'in Dynasty as a defense against barbarian troops from the Mongolian Plateau who periodically invaded the areas of China proper to the south. In terms of geography, the Great Wall can be regarded as the border line separating the moist land and agrarian cultural area of eastern Asia from parched, nomadic inner Asia. Protected by the Great Wall, the Chinese people established a great, highly sophisticated and cultured empire in the south. On the northern side of the Great Wall, on the Mongolian Plateau, a powerful nomadic empire developed.

These two empires did not enjoy peaceful relationships. The Mongols wanted to trade with China, to fill material needs that spelled the difference between life and death. Shortages of supplies constantly threatened the nomadic people. But such trade also gave rise to opportunities for attack. As a result, Chinese emperors made it a rule to send powerful armies to pacify the border areas and to weaken the Tartar tribes whenever they threatened the peace of China proper. Thus, these two powers repeatedly waged cruel wars across the Great Wall. It is no exaggeration to say that, in a sense, the history of East Asia evolved in the process of these conflicts.

An interesting characteristic of the fighting between these two empires is that they usually avoided any decisive, frontal battle. Instead, they aimed primarily, by securing the east and west wings—the area of Manchuria and Korea, and the Sinkiang area, respectively—under their control, to secure strategically superior positions. These east and west wings were naturally regarded as important prizes by both sides.

Manchuria and Korea, open to the influences of the two empires by such circumstances, had the advantage of easy contact with the more highly developed cultures of both northern Asia and mainland China. On the other hand, they could not escape from a very disadvantageous and unhappy situation. Whenever a powerful political force rose in northern Asia, Manchuria and Korea had to kowtow to it; and, in turn, when Chinese strength was the greater, they were forced to submit to its control. Both northern and southern empires wanted to dominate this area for their own benefit, at the expense of the natives. And neither Korea nor Manchuria was strong enough to resist such domination. They actually were dependent on the greater powers for their very survival.

The relationship between Korea and foreign powers is discernible from her very first mention in recorded history. At the beginning of the second century B. C., the first historically authenticated Korean kingdom was established. Called Chosōn, it was a colonial country ruled mainly by Chinese immigrants. In those days the major powers in East Asia were the Mongol Hsung Nu empire and the Han empire of China. The Hsung Nu empire was putting strong pressure on the Han, and Chosōn was caught in the middle of their power struggle. Later, when the Han began to gain ascendancy and was able to subdue the Hsung Nu, it also attacked Chosōn, which finally gave way to Han's superior force in 108 B. C. The Chinese dynasty's rule over Korea, especially over the northwestern part, lasted for more than 420 years. During this period, the Chinese established several colonies in North Korea, the most famous being Lo-lang, with its capital at Pyōngyang.

Chinese rule ended in 313 A. D. During the latter half of the fourth century, the southern kingdoms of native Koreans, Paekche and Silla, were established, although they were under pressure from new foreign powers. The pressure came, on one side, from Koguryo, which had been established in Manchuria; and, on the other, from Japan, which had occupied part of South Korea. The entire fifth century was marked by fighting between these two powers for the control of Korea.

In the middle of the sixth century, Korea entered a period of balance of the three kingdoms: Koguryo in the north, and Paekche and Silla in the south. Koguryo allied itself with the great empire of the Mongolian Plateau, the Turcomans, while the two southern kingdoms, Paekche and Silla, were dependent on China. Koguryo and its friendly relationship with the nomads must have appeared an unpleasant threat to the Chinese rulers. In fact, when China was unified by the Sui and afterward by the T'ang empire, the emperors sent forces to conquer Koguryo. After defeating Paekche in 663 A. D., the T'ang at last occupied Koguryo successfully in 668 A. D., and northern Korea came once again under Chinese control.

Silla, the lone independent kingdom remaining, established a unified country on the peninsula for the first time. At the time of the T'ang withdrawals, however, even Silla was not a securely independent kingdom. It was still protected and supervised by the Chinese.

At the beginning of the tenth century, when the Silla Dynasty collapsed and Koryo established a unified empire in Korea, the political situation grew more complex. At first, the power of the Chinese Sung Dynasty predominated, and the Koryo rulers, admirers of Chinese culture, were willing subjects. Toward the end of the tenth century, however, the situation on the Continent changed. When the Liao from east Mongolia grew powerful, they put pressure on Koryo and attempted to use it to attack the Chinese. Koryo was forced to betray her old master, Sung China. Afterward, the Kin took the place of the Liao as new masters of Koryo, and by the middle of the thirteenth century Koryo became part of the Mongol empire. Mongol domination was very harsh, and Koryo was treated as a colony.

Kingdoms on the Korean peninsula before the Yi Dynasty (1392–1910) were completely at the mercy of either of the two major Asian empires, which held the balance of power. Even the Yi were scarcely independent. Among the countries of eastern Asia, it was customary to choose the new name of an era and to adopt a new calendar on the accession of each new king, actions that symbolized independence. But Korea—although there were some exceptions—usually did not have era names or calendars of its own. Generally, Koreans used the ones given by their masters in China or northern Asia. Even the name *Chaosen*, which the Yi Dynasty used, had to be approved by the Chinese Ming Dynasty before official adoption. This can be partly explained by the fact that the rulers of Korea tried to establish their own authority by acknowledging greater powers, but a more basic reason was the very geographical location of the country, which permitted rampant foreign interference in national affairs.

Perhaps the worst result of this type of subservience was that it stimulated still more severe foreign oppression and provided opportunities for Korean rulers to tyrannize and stifle their own people. This situation was responsible for the delays in social and economic development and for the formation of introverted and pessimistic personality traits among the people. In modern times, Europeans and Americans visiting Korea called it the "hermit nation," so impressed were they by these characteristics.

During the latter half of the nineteenth century, when capitalistic powers arose, conflict between China and Japan over Korea replaced the conflict between the Mongolian and Chinese empires. And behind these struggles hovered the shadows of Western capitalism. Finally, Korea lost all claim to an independent identity and was occupied and ruled by Japan from 1910 to 1945. Though this occupation ended at the close of World War II, Korea, now hopelessly divided by yet another conflict between foreign powers, is still unable to claim real national identity and independence.

General History of Korean Art

The most representative items of Korean Stone Age art are remains of earthenware pottery. The style of living which produced such objects was one fairly widespread in that part of Asia; there were many common elements in the Korean, Siberian, and northeastern Asian cultures at this time, and these similarities are reflected in the implements crafted by each group. The earliest Korean pottery, for example, reflects the essentially open-hearted, candid feeling which permeated the art of the entire area. It differs radically in this respect from the earthenware pieces of Jōmon Japan, which are generally complex in shape and have decorative designs which project a slightly mystical, esoteric spirit. Although the means of expressing the simple, natural character found in Korean primitive and Metal Age art underwent a good deal of change in later ages due to political and social upheavals in the country, the qualities themselves remained throughout the course of its art history.

Several trends appeared in the Three Kingdoms period (fourth century–668). The first and most important was that a national art of high quality and tremendous vigor sprang up and developed rapidly. This art was inspired by two factions of society: the religious (Buddhist), and the aristocratic. At the time, the Korean peninsula was divided among Koguryo, Paekche, and Silla, and a general power balance was maintained. These three kingdoms grew and prospered; they ensured their growth and prosperity by continually adopting and absorbing the excellent artistic and cultural traditions of their neighbors.

In the fourth and fifth centuries, however, an indigenous culture with its own special characteristics was rapidly being built. The huge, beautiful, and uniquely designed General's Tomb at Chian, Chilin-sheng, was built around this time and expresses well the new tastes being evolved. The Three Kingdoms period may be considered an era when Korea borrowed heavily, but selectively, from the cultures and artistic traditions which had grown up in the surrounding, more advanced civilizations. Koreans melded these into something essentially their own in the intense energy of a sudden rise to power as a national culture, and created a new art, full of its own special splendor and strong beauty.

The art of the United Silla period emphasized, even more than previous periods, Buddhist art, and art created for the aristocratic class. Buddhist temples, pagodas, and statues were built in and around Kyongju, the capital, and many masterpieces were left to posterity. Included among the remains of stone architecture and stone sculpture from this time, the Pulkuksa Temple and the Sokkulam cave-temple may be counted as excellent examples of Korean Buddhist art. There were, of course, many common elements shared between the Buddhist and aristocratic art forms. One reason for this is that works of Buddhist art were often commissioned by the nobility. The art of the United Silla period was, in short, built on a foundation of old Silla art from the Three Kingdoms period, absorbing Paekche styles and adding to that mixture selective elements from the art of the contemporaneous T'ang Dynasty in China, which represented the peak of development in the eastern Asian art world.

The Koryo period saw the demand grow in the political centers and the outlying regions for artistically conceived and manufactured craft items. Art was diffused tremendously throughout the country, and artistic boundaries were extended. As in previous periods, growth did not stop at religious-oriented art, but extended to sculpture and painting for the homes of the nobility as well. Not only armor, riding ornaments, and dress and body ornaments, but also objects for everyday use were fashioned. This period was one of the first steps in the expansion of art ideas and style to reach all parts of the country rather than merely the governmental centers.

As the Yi Dynasty rose to power, Buddhist art, which had been one of the bases of Koryo art, gradually disappeared from the forefront; in its place the formalistic, resplendent Confucian architecture and affiliated crafts began to appear. And with the materialization of a new bureaucracy to patronize the arts and to encourage formalism, both painting and stone engraving developed along these lines. Paintings in the "style of the *literati*" were particularly numerous.

Stone Age and Ancient Art

It has been speculated that the design of the earliest earthenware pots found in Korea were marked with a tool having comblike teeth; hence the name: earthenware with comb markings. However, it appears that a variety of instruments were used to make a number of distinctive types of patterns. Whatever the type, the method used was approximately the same: some sort of tool was used to etch the design into the dry, unglazed surface of the pot. The predominant design for the body of the vessel was one of horizontal rows of treelike markings. The most important collection of remains of this earthenware was excavated in the central regions of the country.

In the northern part of the country, metals were already being used in the ancient ages. Examples of remains from this time are iron armor, axes, spades, pots, knives, and alloyed weights and balances, which indicate that an agricultural society had been founded.

Two bronze mirrors have also been discovered. One of these is in perfect condition. It is round, with a diameter of approximately four inches. On its back are two button-like protrusions with holes bored through. Inside the seven-faced margin around the edge are markings—lightning patterns over a series of thin straight lines. The mirror is concave, much the way mirrors in the Chou and Han Dynasties in China were made to catch the sun's rays and start fires. The two raised holes on the back are for carrying purposes.

A sword and its halberd were found from the period of the Warring States inscribed with the characters for the twenty-fifth year of Ch'in and a place-name. The sword blade is about twenty inches long, while its handle is four inches long. Both the sword and the halberd are ornamented with a gold and copper alloy leaf. This is one of the earliest of such works so far uncovered. Another ancient art form is seen in the earthen castle at Lo-lang. The castle was lost long ago but conjectures may be made of its original size and shape from the remains of corner-stones, wooden poles, plaster surfaces, and various kinds of roof tiles which have been discovered in the area. Although no painting or sculpture from Korea's oldest periods have come to light, archaeological findings indicate there were various crafts already developed. The most important of these were personal ornaments found in tombs.

Tombs are classified roughly into two groups: wood-lined underground graves, and tomb mounds. The first type was built with staves of wood brought from Mongolia; the other by piling up small rectangular stones and gathering mounds of earth around the piles. The former tombs held two or four coffins as well as the appropriate accompanying burial objects: figures of retainers, articles necessary for daily life, and so on. They were built vertically down into the ground, with straight sides and a flat-surfaced floor. The latter were built tunnel-like into hills and cliffs, with an entrance on the south side. They usually had about four rooms that contained a coffin and various other objects. Their walls were decorated with pictures of people, birds and beasts, and geometric designs.

A great variety of items were included among the burial objects. Quite technically advanced lacquerwares were especially numerous. They often had patterns of delicate lines in green, brown, and yellow on backgrounds of black or red. Some even had gorgeous gold and silver inlays. Copperware, particularly copper bells, have also been excavated, mostly in the Lo-lang tombs. Finally, ceramic pieces held an important position among funerary wares. The most representative so far found are the unglazed wares, of which there are two basic patterns: a round-bottomed white porcelain, and a flat-bottomed earthenware of greenish-black.

The principal relics inside the coffins were personal ornaments, especially buckles of gold and silver manufacture. The gold-crafted belt clasp with dragon crest and jasper inlaid in gold, which was discovered in the number nine tomb at Sokam-ri, exhibits the splendor and brilliance of these pieces.

The Three Kingdoms Period

Among the architectural ruins throughout Korea, there are many Buddhist temples, and sometimes in these one finds Koguryo sculpture. Numerous tombs were built in the area around temples. There were both stone tombs and tomb mounds. By means of the inside construction—which imitated that of a house— and the wall paintings, one can learn much about the stone constructions and architecture of the period. The most striking example of Koguryo stone construction is the General's Tomb, in the northeastern part of the Chian Plain. This is a stone tomb, undoubtedly that of a king, dating from the latter part of the fifth century. Built as a regularly shaped, seven-level pyramid out of beautifully polished hewn stone, its beautiful proportions are everywhere above reproach.

Wall frescoes in the Koguryo tombs were painted in black, white, red, green, and blue on thick, stuccoed walls. There was an artlessness, a simplicity of line, and a very appealing primitive gaucherie in the portrayals of people, birds and animals, geometric shapes and landscapes. These paintings leaned more heavily than before on techniques from the Six Dynasties period in China. As seen in the figures and in the landscapes and war pictures, however, artists were already imitating styles of composition and a treatment of subject matter peculiar to northwest Korea. These works were done by artists who had studied painting in China and had been commissioned to decorate residences in northwest Korea.

In one of the most important of these wall frescoes, writing was discovered which begins with the date Eiwa 13 (a year of the Eastern Ch'in Dynasty, China) and ends with the name Tōju. From this information we know that it was painted in 357 A.D.

During this time there was no change in the technique of painting on stucco, or in portraying figures of the deceased and scenes from his daily life as subject matter. But many advances can be seen in the delineation of figures and in over-all composition. The dancing scenes in Mu-yong Tomb (Tomb of the Dancers, Chian, Chilin-sheng, China) and the wrestling scenes at Kakcho Tomb (Tomb of the Wrestlers, Chian), particularly, show interesting composition of a high degree of skilled artistry. During this period a tendency developed to draw celestial figures on the ceilings of the tombs, in addition to the more worldly scenes on the walls. Beginning in the middle of the sixth century, the importance of the Four Devas (beast figures) increased, and these gradually took over prime positions as subjects for the four walls of the main room.

Many changes took place in painting in the period from the end of the sixth century to the beginning of the seventh. At this time, painting techniques reached full maturity, and both composition and drawing showed great cleverness, skill, and dexterity. The snake and tortoise painting, and the dragon painting in the Woohyonri Tomb (Summo-ri, Kangso-kun, Pyongan-numdo) are superb examples of the graceful and refined work done at this time.

Looking at Paekche tombs we find that even in the graves dug into the ground the ceilings have become domelike. Other tombs similar to those of Koguryo, with stone rooms decorated with wall paintings on stucco or tiled constructions, have been discovered. The smooth, flowing lines of the wall paintings in these tombs are surprisingly advanced. As opposed to the clumsiness and coarseness of earlier paintings drawn on a rough stucco surface, the extravagance, subtle crafts-manship, and sensitive use of beautiful color produced some of the finest painting styles of this refined period.

Silla had two basic tomb styles: one, horizontally dug graves surrounded by piled-up stones; the other, underground graves. Both had stone-lined rooms. The fomer variety predominated on the plains in and around Kyongju, the old capital. These were round tombs in hill-like mounds, the most representative reaching a height of more than twenty-one meters and a diameter of seventy-six meters. Special characteristics of this style of tomb is: (1) holes dug vertically into the ground with straight sides and flat bottoms; (2) wooden planks lining the walls; (3) center placement of the wooden coffin; and (4) funerary accessories placed around the coffin on all four sides. Once a burial ceremony ended, stones carved in a manner resembling brass work were piled up around and above the coffin, and the grave was covered. Stones from riverbeds were then placed on the grave, and fresh earth was shaped into the tomb mound itself. The tombs were very large, and the relics uncovered have been abundant. This type of tomb represented a great improvement over the earlier hillside tombs. Stone rooms remaining from the two basic tomb styles are widespread throughout the former region of Silla, and roads leading away from the tombs to the south also remain. They linked the tomb proper to ancillary buildings made of cracked rectangular stones or riverbed stones. Large stone planks were placed on the ceilings, a characteristic of later period Japanese tombs.

Koguryo's Buddhist sculpture in the later Three Kingdoms period centered around standing and seated figures. Both were placed upon lotus blossoms. While they were imitations of Buddhist images of the Chinese Northern Dynasties style, the results were quite different in feeling.

The alabaster Buddha and the gilt bronze Bodhisattva, both now in the National Museum of Korea, Seoul, and the Buddha and Two Attendants stone relief are examples of the fundamental style of Paekche Buddhist sculpture. Here we see for the first time head and body halos edged with flames, a central lotus design, and the long flowing drapery scarves which were later to become the main characteristics of Buddhist sculpture of Japan's Asuka period (552–645).

In the field of crafts, Koguryo shapes and techniques did not differ significantly from those of Silla and Paekche. Instead of using gray-black roof tiles common in other kingdoms, red-brown ones were favored. The designs of these—lotus blossoms, devil masks and arabesques—have great simplicity and strength. Paekche exported craft traditions and the Buddhist sculpture style to Asuka Japan. One of these craft exports was roof tiles with single lotus designs, such as are found at Shitennō-ji Temple and Hōryū-ji Temple. But probably the most excellent craftwork done at this time, as is evidenced by the riding equipment and arms found in the tombs, was from Silla. The most important pieces of riding equipment were saddles, stirrups, and bridles. Face plates and rump plates crafted in leather have also been discovered. Stirrups with openwork designs were found, as well as saddles of the same style, in the Gold Crown Tomb. Glasswares were also made. Flat-bottomed cups from the Golden Crown Tomb and round-bottomed cups from the Golden Ring Tomb are representative of what was produced in this period. They are greenish-white ware with blue, wavelike patterns and jewel inlays. A cobalt blue color was added in other instances, and some examples had thick, round drops in relief on the body.

The Unified Silla Dynasty

Buddhist sculpture in the Unified Silla Dynasty (668–935) reveals a strong T'ang influence even while showing special Korean characteristics. Sculpture materials used include gold, silver, copper, iron, tile, and stone. Stone sculpture is broken down further into works done in the round, in relief, and in line engraving. Literary references occasionally mention wood, lacquer, and stucco also being used as materials, but no works in these materials have come down to us.

Stone and gilt bronze Buddhist images predominate in the early Unified Silla period (668–795), while iron-made works appear more numerous later. No matter what the material, however, productions cover a wide range of subjects, and are all shapes and sizes. An image done in stone, for example, might stand forty or fifty feet high, yet another in gilt bronze could easily be life-size or even as little as four inches long. Most iron images are three to ten feet in height. Gilt bronze images only inches long are especially numerous and turn up frequently even today in large temples and at excavation sites. A Korean archaeologist recently excavated twenty-five such Unified Silla images while digging at a temple site. One theory advanced to account for the production of so many small gilt bronze images is that the aristocracy commissioned large quantities of them to affirm their religious sincerity. Though this theory may not be completely valid, it certainly is true that any specialist in Korean art who hears the words "Buddha images of Unified Silla" immediately calls to mind these tiny, gilt bronze works.

Early Unified Silla sculpture other than Buddhist images is represented by the tortoise stele (dated 661), a portion of a dragon-shaped monument that stood before the tomb of King Thae Chog. The stele served as the monument's pedestal, and the bottom section of the dragon is visible on the tortoise's back. While such monuments appear frequently before tombs in T'ang China, no T'ang work of identical age matches this powerful work in elegance and symmetry. In sharp contrast to the T'ang-inspired tortoise stele, tiles such as the green glazed one (found in a Kyongju temple) that depicts in relief the four Deva kings, show how Silla artisans raised the level of ceramic art after importing it from China. A great many tiles excavated at Kyongju depict ogres' faces, phoenixes and other animals, arabesques and similar designs with elegant delicacy. These tiles surpassed all other tiles in the world of the seventh century.

The quality of sculpture, particularly of works done in gilt bronze, deteriorated noticeably during the Unified Silla period. In fact, no outstanding sculpture in bronze has been uncovered. In quantity, too, the number of bronzes falls off sharply. Iron sculptures, on the other hand, display a vigor in the late Silla period suggesting a renewed T'ang influence. The fact that works done in iron predominate in the late Silla period suggests depletion of the peninsula's copper resources. If those resources were depleted, then it follows that even when copper was available, it probably was extremely expensive and therefore scarcely used.

T'ang styles directly influenced Korean sculpture in the late sixth and seventh centuries and helped advance Korean sculpture to its Golden Age. Gradual degeneration after the seventh century, however, suggests that Silla sculpture followed a course nearly identical to the development and decline of T'ang sculpture. Still, on the whole, sculpture of the Unified Silla period reached high technical and quality levels, as proven by the world-famous Buddhist images in Sokkulam, a middle-eighth century cave-temple built close to the summit of Mount Toham in Kyongju. Actually, Sokkulam is an artificial structure built on the slope of, not inside, Mount Toham. A circular main chamber and a rectangular vestibule comprise the temple. The main chamber is about twenty-six feet across and thirty feet high. A white granite figure of a seated Buddha-a huge, sixteen-foot-high statue—occupies the central position in the main chamber. Surrounding the Buddha image are fifteen standing figures (ten disciples and five Bodhisattvas) sculpted in high relief on separate stone slabs set into the chamber wall. Each stone slab is about ten feet in height. Higher up around the chamber wall are ten niches to hold ten seated Devas. The carefully planned design, which focuses attention on the central figure, and the total harmony of the Buddha with the surrounding images contribute to make Sokkulam a true masterpiece of the sculptor's art.

The Buddha image of Sokkulam, with its symmetry and over-all refinement of expression and pose, represents the very zenith of Silla sculpture. The beholder senses an ethereal beauty in moment to moment changes that take place in the Buddha's countenance as the dawn sun strikes it. The high relief image of the goddess Kannon, located just beyond the main Buddha image, displays an elegance closely akin to small Kannon images in Hōryū-ji Temple in Nara, Japan. The similarity is not just coincidental but speaks for the proliferation of T'ang culture throughout Asia.

Together with the spread of Buddhism and its adoption as the official state religion, many temples were built throughout the country. The large number of mountain temples suggests a geomantic belief that a temple or temples favorably influenced surrounding areas. In particular, groups of temples have been found in the hills south of Kyongju, the old capital. Pulkuksa Temple, on the slope of a mountain in eastern Kyongju, like so many other Silla period temples, was originally wood and succumbed to the ravages of age. Wooden structures such as the main hall of Pulkuksa date from a period of reconstruction following Hideyoshi's invasions from Japan in the late sixteenth century.

The pagoda is an essential feature of Buddhist temples that houses a relic of Buddha. The earliest Korean pagodas were probably wooden copies of Chinese originals. They gave way early in the seventh century to stone pagodas, first of all in Paekche. In the Unified Silla Dynasty, artisans combined styles and characteristics of the old wooden and the new stone pagodas to produce a unique Korean structure known as the Silla pagoda. A typical Silla pagoda is three-or five-storied and is set on a double pedestal, the upper pedestal usually thicker than the lower. Each story is successively smaller and narrower than the preceding one, and a decorative finial tops the last story. The earliest pagodas were built using many pieces of stone in each section. Gradually, however, each story came to be comprised of two blocks of stone: the main stone and the roof stone. The roof stone is almost always curved, and often has turned-up corners. Steplike supporting stones between the main and the roof stones show a striking Chinese influence.

Since most pagodas dating from the Silla period have lost their finials, the extremely rare, almost perfect finials of the twin, three-storied pagodas of Shilsangsa Temple (middle ninth century) are veritable treasures. As demonstrated by these two pagodas, finials generally comprised a large proportion of a pagoda's total height.

A variation on the common type of pagoda is one that utilizes sculpture. The lion pagoda at Hwaohmsa Temple is a very fine example. Four lions—or, rather, lion-like animals—seated, and facing outward, are set on the second tier of the pedestal in caryatid fashion to support the pagoda's upper stories. A human figure stands between the lions—in the direct center under the first roof stone —and engraved doors on the four sides of the first main stone are protected by the lions. High relief sculptures of twelve Devas decorate the pedestal on all sides immediately below the lions. The steplike stones between the main and the roof stones, the turned-up corners of the eaves, and the finial are much like the common type of Silla pagoda. This lion pagoda, which has no extant precedents, represents the tendency in the middle eighth to late ninth century to integrate sculpture into a pagoda.

Two other variations are the rare, tiled-roof pagodas of the late Silla period and a thirteen-storied pagoda at Chonghesa Temple, which from the second story up is comprised of roof stones and no main stones. The first roof stone is quite large while the second and succeeding ones taper off quickly to give the overall impression of a tower. This is the only thirteen-storied pagoda existing in Korea.

A last variation is the so-called Prabhutaratna pagoda of Pulkuksa Temple in Kyongju. Completed in the ninth century, it is one of the real masterpieces of Silla stonework. Some authorities consider it an enlarged version of an earlier piece of bronze art, while others prefer to stress the architectural details that are so faithful to earlier wooden structures.

Archaeological remains of the Silla period include mausoleums, tumuli, pottery, ceramics, and bells. Perhaps the most representative tomb is that of King Thae Chog. Korean sculpture advanced markedly after reunification, and tombs, formerly located on the plains, came to be constructed on mountains and hills. In T'ang fashion, stone statues of men (court officials, attendants, and so on) and protective animals, and of the twelve Korean zodiacal signs, either lined approaches or were placed before tombs. Hundreds of such sculptures have been passed down to us.

A large number of Korean temple bells from the Unified Silla period still exist in Korea and Japan. Their high quality speaks for the tremendous advances made in Korean metal craft during the Silla era. The best example of a bell is the one preserved in the Kyongju Branch of the National Museum, a bell cast for King Sondok and completed in 707 A.D. It stands eleven feet high, is seven and a half feet in diameter, and required between seventy and eighty tons of bronze for casting. The mouth of the bell is octagonal, while the lower outside surface is decorated with a double-petaled lotus flower design. A single, large lotus flower design also decorates and marks the spot for striking the bell. Still more lotus and other decorative designs are cast in relief on the upper part of the bell. Flying devata in relief serve as beautiful line designs on either side of the bell's striking point. The King Sondok bell expresses the quintessence of Unified Silla metalwork and is one of the most famous Chosŏn bells.

It has been put that of Chinese, Japanese, and Korean art the former two are like court ladies who appear attractive largely because of makeup and gorgeous costumes, while the latter is like an everyday housewife who wears plain clothes and sometimes looks tired but who, nevertheless, has a beauty that sparkles from inside, a kind of philosophy that surrounds her very being.

The Koryo Period

In the Koryo period (935–1392), Buddhist sculpture was initially a continuation of Unified Silla traditions. Sung and Yüan influences appeared from the middle to the late Koryo period. Buddhism itself grew gradually more decadent as the Koryo era progressed, and the demand for Buddha images declined. Great Buddhist ceremonies were still conducted by the state—literature mentions frequent gatherings at formal ceremonies with twenty to thirty thousand priests—but the ceremonies only served to emphasize the formalism that had crept into the religion. Moreover, the spread of Pure Land and Zen Buddhism, both of which disregard ritual, led to a further decrease in the demand for images. This combination of reasons accounts for there being no truly outstanding Buddhist sculpture in Koryo. The Buddha images that were made are severely lacking in divinity. In effect, Koryo inherited from the Unified Silla period not the art but the techniques of Buddhist sculpture. In the thirteenth century, Koryo was influenced by Yüan China, whose official religion was Lamaism. Work eventually became so roughshod that it is sometimes likened to the doll-making craft.

Materials used throughout Koryo in sculpture are gilt bronze, iron, stucco, and stone. The creation of huge Buddha images in stone is a special characteristic of Koryo sculpture that is even unusual in the history of world sculpture. Another peculiarity of Koryo Buddhist sculpture is the existence of a large number of seated images, a posture radically different from the standing figures of the Unified Silla era. No theory has been put forward to account for this change. The finest example of a seated Buddhist image, and the most technically perfect of Buddha sculpture produced in Koryo, is the fourth-century stucco (painted clay-over-wood) Amitahba statue in Pusok-sa Temple.

Of all the huge stone images dating from early Koryo the best example is the image of Maitreya in Kwangchok-sa Temple. Standing sixty-five feet high, it is the largest Buddhist statue on the Korean peninsula. While neither the Maitreya image nor any of the other stone Buddhist sculptures that stand twenty to thirty feet high have much artistic merit, their size is suggestive of great vitality. In no manner of speaking, however, do they measure up to Silla productions.

No discussion of Korean art would be complete without discussing the "secret colored" celadon wares that in the tenth century surprised even highly cultured Chinese visitors to Korea. Korean celadons are world renowned and praised as "one of those rare types of art wherein chemistry and the formative spirit of human beings were highly and completely harmonized."

Celadon techniques probably came to the south and southwestern coast of Korea directly across the sea from Sung China. The mainstream of celadon production, at any rate, was always in the extreme southwest, and it was there that these wares developed from the late tenth to the early twelfth centuries. Development followed a cycle: an initial transitional stage, an imitative stage, an interlude during which purely indigenous approaches and style developed, a mature stage, and then decline. Of that total period, a vast number of celadons were produced and covered a wide range of colors, techniques, shapes, and designs. Celadons have been placed in fifteen general categories. The most important by far is that of the green glazed ware. Its elegant shapes, the beauty of its slender, curved lines, and its wonderful glaze became the model of Koryo esthetic taste.

Korean celadons preserved in Japan include some of the most beautiful of the green glazed ware. The earliest of these came to Japan during the Kamakura period and were passed from generation to generation in such great houses as the Nezu and Honma families. By far the largest number of green celadons, however— literally thousands of pieces—were carried or traded to Japan after Japanese rule of Korea began in 1909 A. D. Japanese-instigated excavations and bartering that centered around the green celadons subsided only after the government intervened and issued a prohibition in the late Meiji period. By that time most of the high quality ware had probably been unearthed.

The most outstanding celadon collections are in Korea, followed by Japanese collections such as the one in the Nezu Museum in Tokyo. Celadons in Japan have been discovered in Fukuoka, Kamakura, and parts of Hiroshima Prefecture. Some celadon ware exists in the United States, and a small number of pieces are in

Europe.

The Yi Dynasty

The Yi Dynasty (1392–1910) covers one of the most settled periods in Korean history. Lamaism, introduced at the end of the thirteenth century from Yüan China, gave way to Confucianism early in the Yi period, a development which spelled the doom of Buddhism and completely halted Korea's sculptural development.

After Confucianism was adopted as the state religion, a cultural movement erupted which led to remarkable advances in many fields of Korean art. While Yi painting contains influences from Sung, Yüan, and Ch'ing China, and from the *suiboku* (water ink) paintings of Japan, most of the work displays indigenous characteristics and uses more indigenous techniques than earlier Korean art. A great demand arose for portraits of kings, national figures, aristocrats, and even for the deceased, for purposes of veneration. The terrific demand precipitated rapid progress in the field of painting.

Professional painters were mostly members of the government sponsored Office of Arts. Other professionals formed another circle of artists that included scholars, writers, political figures, and members of the intelligentsia who painted as amateurs. A representative early Yi Dynasty painter is the great landscape artist An Kyon who worked in the northern style of Sung and Yüan China, especially close to the Chinese master Kwak Hi. He was a member of the Office of Arts and a close companion to the son of King Se Jong. In his "Visit in a Dream to T'ao-Yüan," done in ink and faint color on silk, he unfolds before us his creative imagination and delicate grasp of description.

We must remember that An Kyon and most other artists worked in rather aristocratic settings. They greatly admired Chinese painting and seldom made any effort to break from subject or technical traditions to realize an individuality or peculiar Korean style. Two exceptions were Sun Chung and Hong Do Kim. Chung adopted techniques of his own even while being influenced by Ming and Ch'ing paintings. Although he displayed great talent as a landscape artist, no other Korean painter adopted either his techniques or brush methods. Kim, born in 1760 A.D. was most active at the end of the eighteenth and beginning of the nineteenth centuries. He was a member of the Office of Arts but cultivated genre paintings which depicted with irony various aspects of the commoner's life. He excelled in works portraying fairies and has left equally good masterpieces of landscapes. He occupies a special position in the history of Korean painting for his ability to work effectively with subjects ranging from the lowest to the highest levels of society.

The practical ideas of Confucianism influenced Korean handicrafts greatly. All works in the minor arts and crafts seemed to take on a nonaristocratic, practical beauty. In ceramics, the celadons of Koryo declined gradually to be replaced by a light greenish-blue pottery called Punchong. Punchong became extinct after Hideyoshi's invasions from Japan at the end of the sixteenth century. Meanwhile, white porcelains derived from Koryo and from Ming China, became increasingly refined and are seen throughout all of the Yi period.

Glossary

earthenware with comb markings : Rustic, unglazed pottery of Korea's Stone Age on which straight or dotted lines were etched by using a comb-shaped instrument.

Four Devas : In ancient China, constellations were considered to be gods governing the four directions. The constellations were given animal names to fit their shapes. The Four Devas correspond to these animals. During the Koguryo dynasty the Four Devas were a main theme of wall paintings.

> East : blue dragon
> West : white tiger
> North : black snake-tortoise
> South : red phoenix

General's Tomb : A representative tomb of Korea's Koguryo period.

kangōsen : Japanese government vessels of the Muromachi period that traded products from Ming China and Korea.

Koguryo : One of three powerful states in old Korea. It occupied the northern part of the peninsula and extended into Manchuria. With Koguryo's defeat in 668 by T'ang China, all of Korea came under Chinese control. Koguryo was important especially for its role in transmitting Chinese culture of the Northern Dynasty. Frescoes in Koguryo tombs reflect the peculiar circumstances of the period.

Lo-lang : The best-known Chinese colony established in northern Korea after Han China defeated Chōson (Korea) in 108. Han China's influence was especially strong from 108 to 313. A number of tumuli remain from that period.

magatama : Curved or claw-shaped beads usually made of glass, rock crystal, amber or agate. They were used for body ornamentation.

Mishima type : A type of pottery popular during the fifteenth century in Korea. Tea masters of Japan were especially fond of this pottery.

Paekche : A state of Korea's Three Kingdoms period. It existed until 663 in the southwestern part of the peninsula. In the cultural area, Paekche was influenced greatly by the Six Dynasties of China. It served as intermediary in introducing that culture to Japan.

punchong : A light, greenish-blue pottery.

Silla : One state of Korea's Three Kingdoms period. About the middle of the seventh century Silla joined with T'ang China to defeat Koguryo and Paekche, and was the predominant Korean state until 935. The Silla period resulted in a large number of masterpieces in Buddhist and aristocratic art.

Turcomans : A great empire of the Mongolian Plateau.

wakō : A name given by Chinese and Koreans to Japanese smugglers who worked the Chinese mainland and the Korean peninsula from the thirteenth to the sixteenth centuries.

Korea—All Periods from Ancient to Modern.

1 Bronze Tube with Gold and Silver Inlay.
Lolang Period. From a Tomb at Pyongyang.

2 Buckle. Filigree Work. Lolang Period. From a Tomb
at Pyongyang. National Museum of Korea, Seoul.

3 Box Painted with Colored Lacquer (Side View). Lolang Period.
From Chaehyob Tomb at Pyongyang. Historical Museum of
Korea, Pyongyang.

4 Desk Painted with Colored Lacquer (Top Surface). Lolang
Period. From Chaehyob Tomb at Pyongyang. National
Museum of Korea, Seoul.

5 Lacquered Tray. Lolang Period. From Wang Kwang Tomb
at Pyongyang. National Museum of Korea, Seoul.

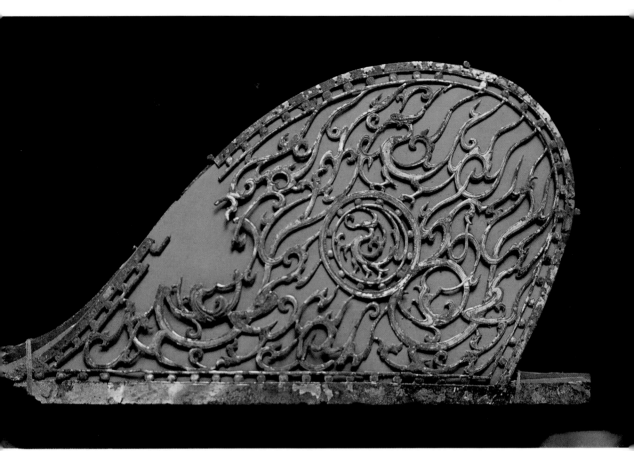

6 Gilt Bronze Openwork Fitting. Koguryo Dynasty. From Tomb No. 1, Chinpa-ri, Chunghwa-kun, Pyongan-numdo. Historical Museum of Korea, Pyongyang.

7   Hsüan-wu (Snake-tortoise). Wall-painting in Great
    Tomb of Woohyon-ri. Koguryo Dynasty. Summo-ri,
    Kangso-kun, Pyongan-numdo.

8   Ts'ang-lung (Dragon). Wall-painting in Great Tomb of Woohyonri.
    Koguryo Dynasty. Summo-ri, Kangso-kun, Pyongan-numdo.

9   Wrestling Scene. Wall-painting
     in Kakcho Tomb (Wrestlers).
     Koguryo Dynasty. Chian, Chilin-
     shêng, China.

10 Chu-chüeh (Phoenix). Wall-painting
     in Middle Tomb of Woohyon-ri.
     Koguryo Dynasty. Summo-ri,
     Kangso-kun, Pyongan-numdo.

11 Master of a House. Wall-painting in Tomb No. 3, Anak. 12 Housewife. Wall-painting in Tomb No. 3, Anak.
    Koguryo Dynasty. Anak-kun, Hwanghae-numdo.   Koguryo Dynasty. Anak-kun, Hwanghae-numdo.

13 Procession Scene. Wall-painting in Tomb No. 3, Anak.
Koguryo Dynasty. Anak-kun, Hwanghae-numdo.

14 Hunting Scene. Wall-painting in Mu-yong Tomb
(Tomb of the Dancers) . Koguryo Dynasty. Chian,
Chilin-shêng, China.

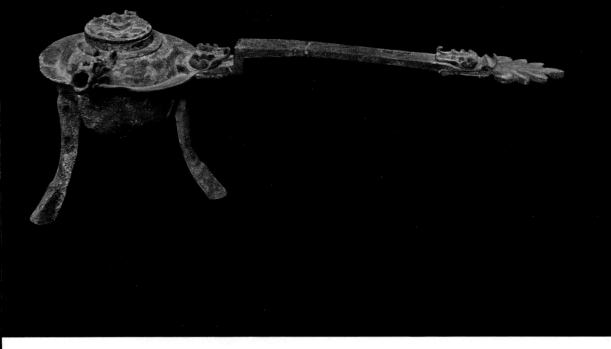

15 Incense Burner with Long Handle. Bronze. Old Silla
Dynasty. From Koomkwan Tomb, Kyongsang-pukdo.
Kyonju Branch of National Museum of Korea, Kyonju.

16 Wall-painting in a Tomb (Copy). Paekche Dynasty.
Noongsan-ri, Puyo-kun, Chungchong-numdo.

17 Bodhisattva in Meditative Pose. Gilt Bronze. Paekche
Dynasty. National Museum of Korea, Seoul.

18 Bodhisattva in Meditative Pose (Detail). Gilt Bronze.
Paekche Dynasty. Toksu Palace Museum, Seoul.

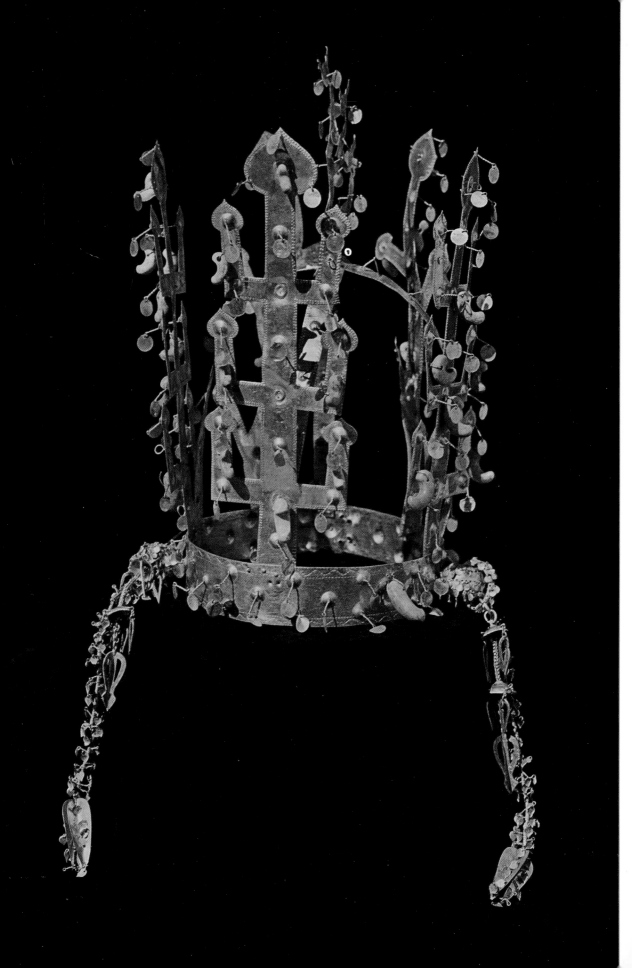

20　Tile with Image of One of Four Heavenly Kings,
　　Yellowgreen Glaze. Great Silla Dynasty. From the
　　Ruins of Green wang-sa Temple, Kyongsang-pukdo.
　　National Museum of Korea, Seoul.

19　Gold Crown. Old Silla (Three Kingdoms Period)
　　Dynasty. From Sobong Tomb, Kyongsang-pukdo.
　　National Museum of Korea, Seoul.

21 Stone Pagoda of Punhwan-sa Temple. 634.
Suburbs of Kyongju, Kyongsang-pukdo.

22   Pulkuksa Temple. Great Silla Dynasty.
     Kyongju, Kyongsang-pukdo.

23 Cinerary Urn, Yellow Glaze. Great Silla
Dynasty. From Suburbs of Kyonju.
National Museum of Korea, Seoul.

24 Covered Circular Box with
Arabesque Design in
Mother-of-Pearl Inlay.
Koryo Dynasty. Taima-
dera Temple, Nara.

25 Incense Burner with Ara-
besque Design in Silver Inlay.
Koryo Dynasty. Historical
Museum of Korea, Pyongyang.

26 Ewer and Stand, with Openwork Design of Lotus
Scrolls, Celadon. Koryo Dynasty. National Museum
of Korea, Seoul.

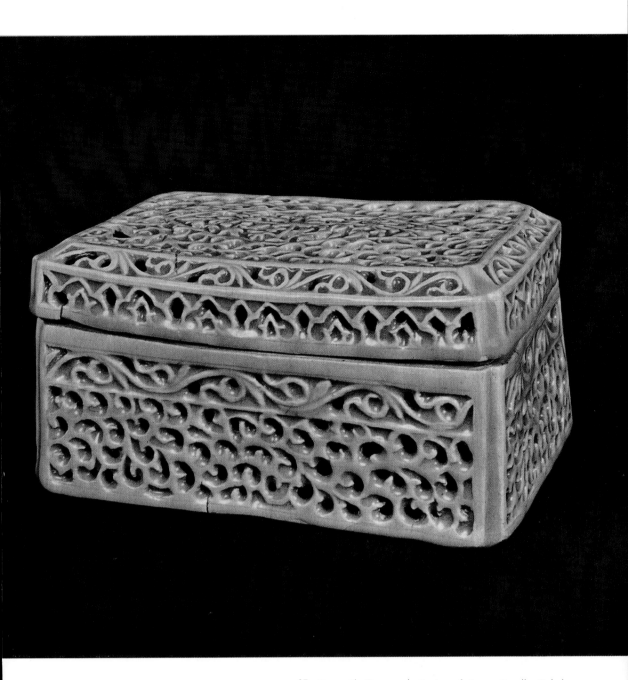

27 Box with Openwork Design of Peony Scrolls, Celadon.
Koryo Dynasty. National Museum, Tokyo.

28 Gourd-shaped Ewer with Lotus Petal
Design, Celadon with Underglaze Red.
Koryo Dynasty.

29 Ewer with Engraved Lotus Scroll
Design, Celadon. Koryo Dynasty.
Nezu Art Museum, Tokyo.

30 Avalokiteśvara with Willow Branch. By Hye Ho.
Koguryo Dynasty. Sensō-ji Temple, Tokyo.

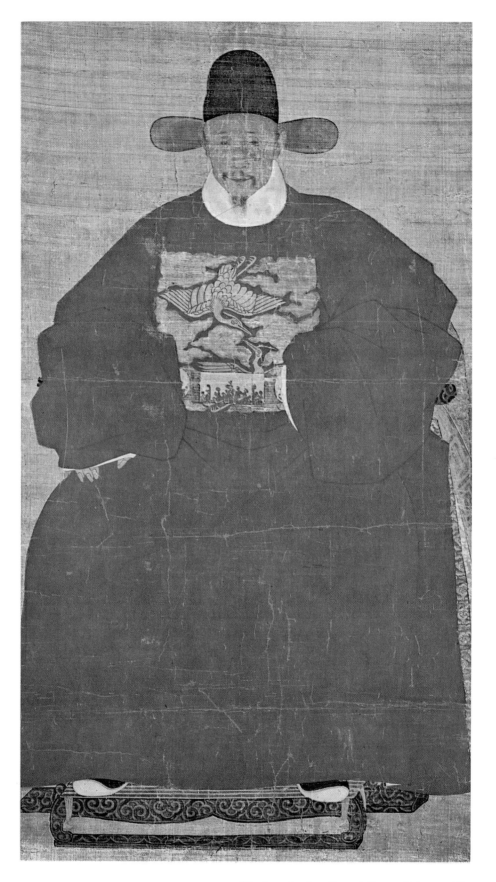

31 Portrait of a King of Korea. Color on Silk.
Yi Dynasty. Sōan-ji Temple, Hikone.

32 Flask, "Engraved Mishima" Type.
Ceramics. Yi Dynasty.

33 Vase with Lotus and Willow Design,
"Mishima" Type. Ceramics. Early
Yi Dynasty.

34 Water Dropper with Figure
Design, Blue and White with
Coppered. Ceramics. Yi Dynasty.

35 Bevelled Jar, Underglaze
Coppered. Ceramics.
Yi Dynasty.

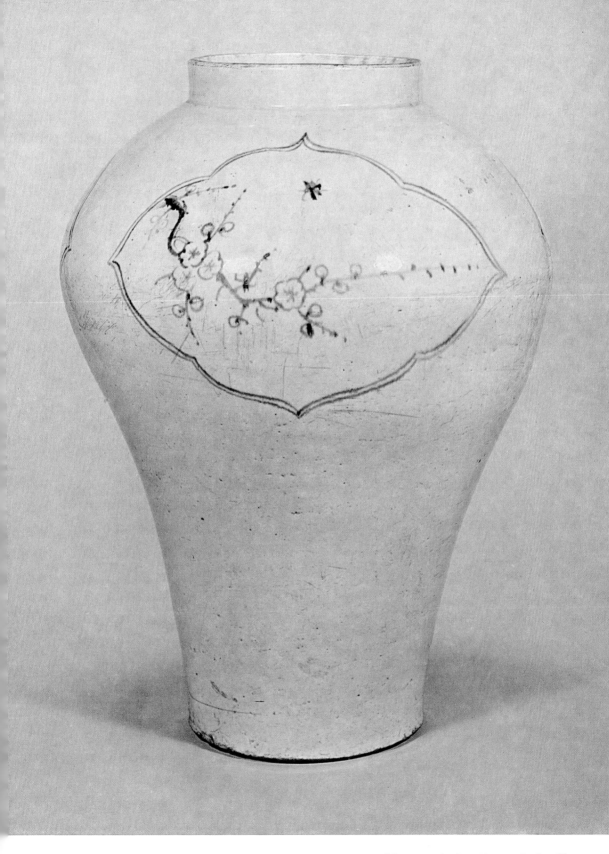

36 Jar with Plum Blossom Design, Blue and White. Ceramics. Yi Dynasty.

37 Smoking-set Box with Silver
Inlay. Yi Dynasty. Japan
Folk Craft Museum, Tokyo.

38 Box Covered with Sliced Horn. Yi
Dynasty. National Museum, Tokyo.

1 Earthenware with Comb-mark Patterns. Stone Age. From Yomdo-ri, Yongung-kun, Pyongan-numdo. Kyoto University, Kyoto.

2 Jar with Painted Ornament. Stone Age. From near
Lake Yongsu, Woonggi-kun, Hamgyong-pukdo.

Spouted Vessel. Stone Age. From Yongson-
don Kitchen Midden at Pusan.

4   Earthenware with Comb-mark Patterns.
Stone Age. From Yongson-don Kitchen
Midden at   Pusan.

5 Roof Tiles. Lolang Period. From Pyongyang.
Tokyo University, Tokyo.

6 Shoulder-piece with Hunting-scene Design. Bronze.
Calcolithic Age. From near Kyongiu.

7 Ting (Tripod). Earthenware. Lolang Period. From
Pyongyang. Tokyo University, Tokyo.

8 Clay Seals. Lolang Period. From
Pyongyang. Tokyo University,
Tokyo.

9 Tou (Stem Bowl). Earthenware. Lolang
Period. From Pyongyang. Tokyo
University, Tokyo.

10 Guard of Spear, Iron. Lolang Period. From Sokam-ri, Pyongyang. National Museum of Korea, Seoul.

11 Horse, Wood. Lolang Period. From the Tomb of Painting Basket at Pyongyang. National Museum of Korea, Seoul.

12 Incense Burner with "Hill" Cover. Bronze. Lolang Period. From a Tomb at Pyongyang. National Museum of Korea, Seoul.

13 Jade Pi (Ritual Disk). Lolang Period. From a Tomb at Pyongyang. National Museum of Korea, Seoul.

14 Mirror with Design of Figure Subjects and Inscription
"Shang-fang". Bronze. Lolang Period. From a Tomb
at Pyongyang. National Museum of Korea, Seoul.

15 Shogun-zuka (General's Tomb). Koguryo Dynasty.
Chian, Chilin-shêng, China.

16 Procession Scene. Wall-painting in Tomb No. 12, Chian.
Koguryo Dynasty, Chian, Chilin-shêng, China.

Kitchen Scene. Wall-painting in Tomb No. 3, Anak. Koguryo Dynasty. Anak-kun, Hwanghae-numdo.

18 Procession Scene. Wall-painting in Tomb No. 3, Anak, Koguryo Dynasty, Anak-kun, Hwanghae-numdo.

20 Taoistic Immortal. Wall-painting in Sashin Tomb(Tomb of
the Four Spirits). Koguryo Dynasty. Chian, Chilin-shêng,
China.

9 Arabesque. Wall-painting in Sashin Tomb (Tomb of the Four Spirits). Koguryo Dynasty. Chian, Chilin-shêng, China.

21 Hsüan-wu (Snake-tortoise). Wall-painting in Sashin Tomb. (Tomb of the Four Spirits). Koguryo Dynasty. Chian. Chilin-shêng, China.

22 Gilt-bronze Openwork Fitting (Detail). Koguryo Dynasty. From
Tomb No. 1, Chinpa-ri, Chunghwa-kun, Pyongan-numdo.

23 Epitaph for King Hong Thae. Koguryo
Dynasty. Chian, Chilin-shêng, China.

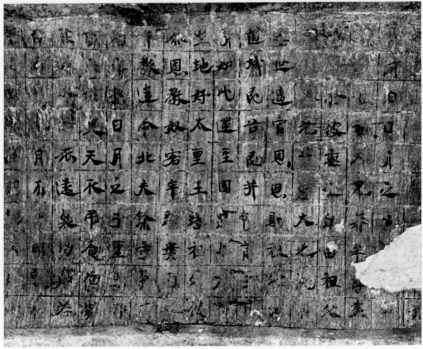

24 Monumental Inscription at Mu Du Ru
Tomb. Koguryo Dynasty. Chian.
Chilin-shêng, China.

25 Tile with Phoenix Design. Paekch
    Dynasty. From Kyuam-myon,
    Puyo-kun, Chungchong-numdo.
    National Museum of Korea, Seou

26 Tile with Arabesque Design.
    Paekche Dynasty. From Kyuam-
    myon, Puyo-kun, Chungchong-nu
    National Museum of Korea,
    Seoul.

27 Tile with Goblin Figure.
Paekche Dynasty, From
Kyuam-myon, Puyo-kun,
Chungchong-numdo.
National Museum of
Korea, Seoul.

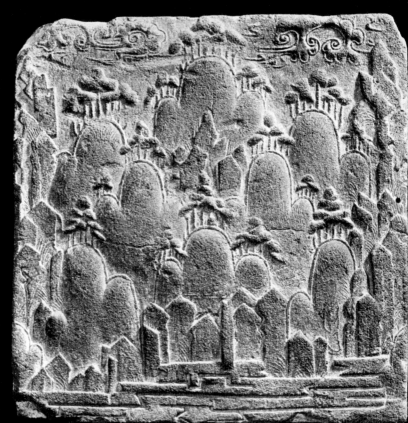

28 Tile with Landscape
Design. Paekche Dynasty.
From Kyuam-myon, Puyo-
kun, Chungchong-numdo.
National Museum of
Korea, Seoul.

29 Tile Burial Chamber and Wall-painting. Paekche Dynasty.
From Sonsun-ri, Kongju-kun, Chungchong-numdo.

30 Boat-shaped Vessel. Old Silla Dynasty. From Kumnyong
(Golden Bell) Tomb, Kyongsang-pukdo.

31 Bodhisattva. Gilt Bronze. Paekche Dynasty.
From Kunsoo-ri, Puyo-kun, Chungchong-numdo.
National Museum of Korea. Seoul.

32 Buddha. Alabaster. Paekche Dynasty. From Kunsoo-ri,
Puyo-kun, Chungchong-numdo. National Museum of
Korea, Seoul.

33 Buddha and Two Attendants. Relief on Rock Cliff. Paekche
Dynasty, Yonghyon-ri, Sosun-kun, Chungchong-numdo.

34 Jar. Old Silla Dynasty. From near Kyongju, Kyongsang-pukdo.

35 Covered Jar with Handle. Old Silla Dynasty. From near Kyongju, Kyongsang-pukdo.

36 Bowl with Tall Foot. Old Silla Dynasty. From near Kyongju, Kyongsang-pukdo.

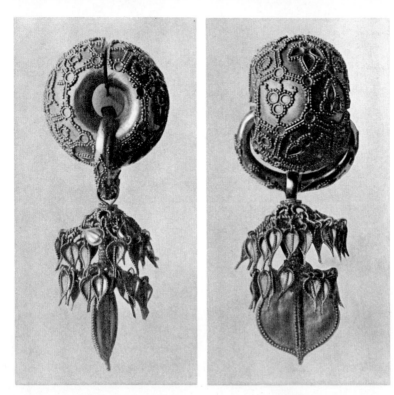

37 Ear-rings with Gold Filigree. Old Silla Dynasty. From a Tomb at Kyongju, Kyongsang-pukdo. National Museum of Korea, Seoul.

38 Head of Buddha. Gilt Bronze. Old Silla Dynasty. From the Ruins of a Temple near Kyongju, Kyongsang-pukdo. Kyongju Branch of National Museum of Korea, Kyongju.

39 Bodhisattva in Meditative Pose. Granite. Old Silla Dynasty. From Sowak-ri.
Kyongju. Kyongju Branch of National Museum of Korea, Kyongju.

40 Bell for King Sondok. Great Silla Dynasty. Kyongju
Branch of National Museum of Korea, Kyongju.

41 Stele at the Tomb of King Thae Chog (Mu Yol).
661. Punae-myon, Kyongsan-pukdo.

42 Bhaisajyaguru. Gilt Bronze. G[...]
Silla Dynasty. Museum of Fin[...]
Arts, Boston.

43 Vairocana. Gilt Bronze. Middle of 8th C. Buddha Hall
of Pulkuk-sa Temple, Chinhyon-ri, Kyongju-kun,
Kyongsang-pukdo.

44 Amitābha. Gold. Early 8th C. Discovered
    in the Stone Three-storied Pagoda on
    the Ruins of Hwangbok-sa Temple,

45 Sākyamuni (Detail). Granite. Middle o
    8th C. Sokkulam Temple, Kyongju,
    Kyongsang-pukdo.

46 Three-storied Pagoda, Shilsang-sa
Temple. Middle of 9th C. Ibbsok-
ri, Sunae-myon, Jolla-pukdo.

47 Pagoda, Pulkuk-sa Temple Middle of 8th C.
Chinhyon-ri, Kyongju-kun, Kyongsang-pukdo

48 Five-storied Pagoda in Hwaohm-sa Temple. End of
9th C. Hwangjon-ri, Masun-myon, Jolla-numdo.

49 Stone Pagoda of Four Lions in Hwaohm-sa Temple. End of
9th C. Hwangjon-ri, Masun-myon, Jolla-numdo.

50 Stone Figures of Monkey (Abov
and Ram (Below). Tomb of a
King, Kyongju. Great Silla Dyno
Oedoong-myon, Kyongsang-puk

51 Stone Figure of Man. Tomb of a King, Kyongju. Great
Silla Dynasty. Oedoong-myon, Kyongsang-pukdo.

52 Vajradhara Engraved on Stone Door. Great Silla Dynasty. Attributed
to a Tomb at Soak-ri, Kyongju, Kyongsang-pukdo. Toksu Palace
Museum, Seoul.

53 Goblin-mask Handles. Bronze. Great Silla Dynasty. Attributed
to a Tomb at Soak-ri, Kyongju, Kyongsang-pukdo. National
Museum of Korea, Seoul.

54 Roof Tiles. Phoenix, Man-birds and Hosoge Flower.
Great Silla Dynasty.

55 Roof Tiles. Heavenly Beings, Arabesque, Birds with
Flowers in the Bills, and Phoenixes. Great Silla Dynasty.

56 Roof Tile with Lotus Flower Design.
Great Silla Dynasty. From the Ruins of
Imhae Palace, Kyongju.

57 Roof Tile with Giraffe Design.
Great Silla Dynasty.

59 Gamoyle. Great Silla Dynas
From the Ruins of a Temple.
Kyongju.

60 Tile with Hōsōge Flower
Design. Great Silla Dynasty.
From the Ruins of Imhae
Palace, Kyongju.

61 Roof Tile with Hunting-scene Design. Great
Silla Dynasty. From Sajong-ri, Kyongju.
National Museum of Korea, Seoul.

62 Sarira Casket of Kamun-sa
Temple. From Youngbok-myon
Kyongsang-pukdo. National
Museum of Korea, Seoul.

63 Cinerary Urn with Stamped
Ornament. Great Silla
Dynasty. From Kyongju,
Kyongsang-pukdo.

64 Head of Buddha. Bronze.
Early Koryo Dynasty.

65 Sākyamuni. Iron. Late Silla~Early Koryo Dynasty.
Koonjyong Palace at Kyongbok Palace, Seoul.

66 Amitābha. Stucco. Koryo Dynasty. Pusok-sa Temple,
Pusok-myon, Kyongsang-pukdo.

67 Maitreya. Stone. Early
Koryo Dynasty.
Kwangchok-sa Temple,
Chungchong-numdo.

68 Mask of Court Servant. Wood. Late
Koryo Dynasty. National Museum of
Korea, Seoul.

69 Bhaisajyaguru. 977. Yaksakok, Kwangju-kun,
Kyonggwi-do.

Memorial Pagoda for Priest
Chi Kwang of Pobchon-sa
Temple. 1085. Kyongbok
Palace, Seoul.

71   Stone Octagonal Nine-
storied Pagoda. Koryo
Dynasty. Wolchong-sa
Temple, Chinpu-myon,
Kangwon-do.

72   Buddha Hall of Soodook-sa Temple (Detail). 1308.
     Dooksun-myon, Chungchong-numdo.

73   Lobed Vase, Celadon. Koryo Dynasty.
     Cleveland Museum of Art, Cleveland.

74 Ewer with Lotus Petal Design in Relief. Celadon. Koryo Dynasty.
Brooklyn Museum New York.

75 Ewer with Engraved Lotus Scroll Design,
Celadon (Detail). Koryo Dynasty. Nezu Art
Museum, Tokyo.

76 Square Incense Burner with Relief Ornament,
Celadon. Koryo Dynasty.

77 Figure of Monkey with
Its Baby, Celadon. Koryo
Dynasty.

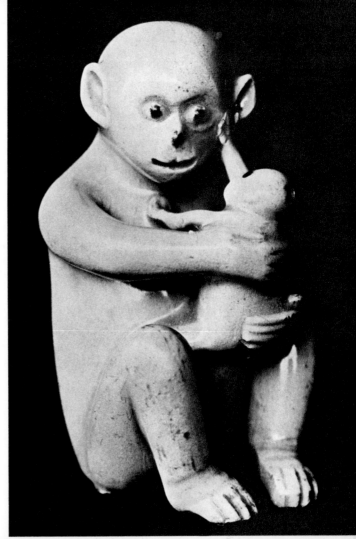

78 Figure of Duck, Celadon.
Koryo Dynasty.

79 Pillow with Lion Supports,
Inlaid Celadon. Koryo Dynasty
Toksu Palace Museum, Seoul.

80 Sherd with Openwork Design of
Interlocking Circles, Celadon. Kor
Dynasty. Cleveland Museum of
Art, Cleveland.

81 Gourd-shaped Ewer and Stand with Child Design,
    Inlaid Celadon with Underglaze Copper Red. Koryo
    Dynasty. Toksu Palace Museum, Seoul.

82 Ewer with Bamboo Design in Underglaze Brown-
black, Celadon. Koryo Dynasty. Art Institute of

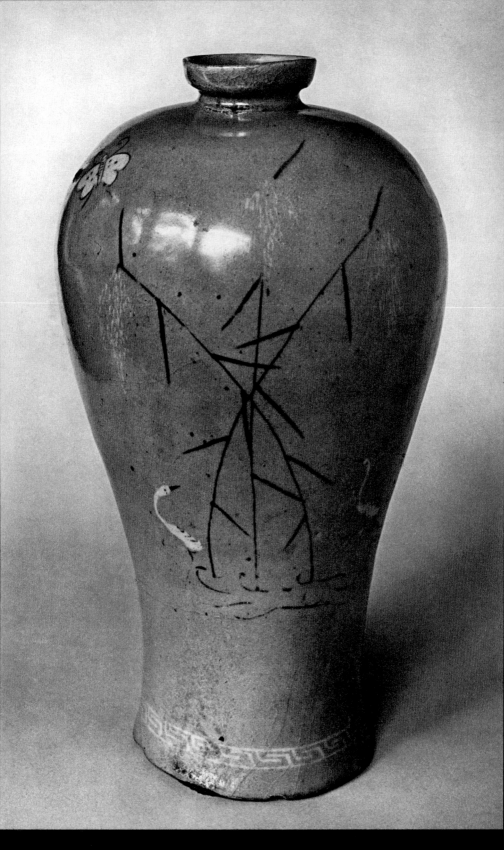

83 Vase with Reed and Heron Design, Inlaid
Celadon. Koryo Dynasty. National Museum,

84 Jar with "Seven Luminaries" Design in
Brown-black, Celadon. Koryo Dynasty.

85 Vase with Flowering Plant Design withi
Reserve Panels, White Ware. Koryo
Dynasty. National Museum of Korea,
Seoul.

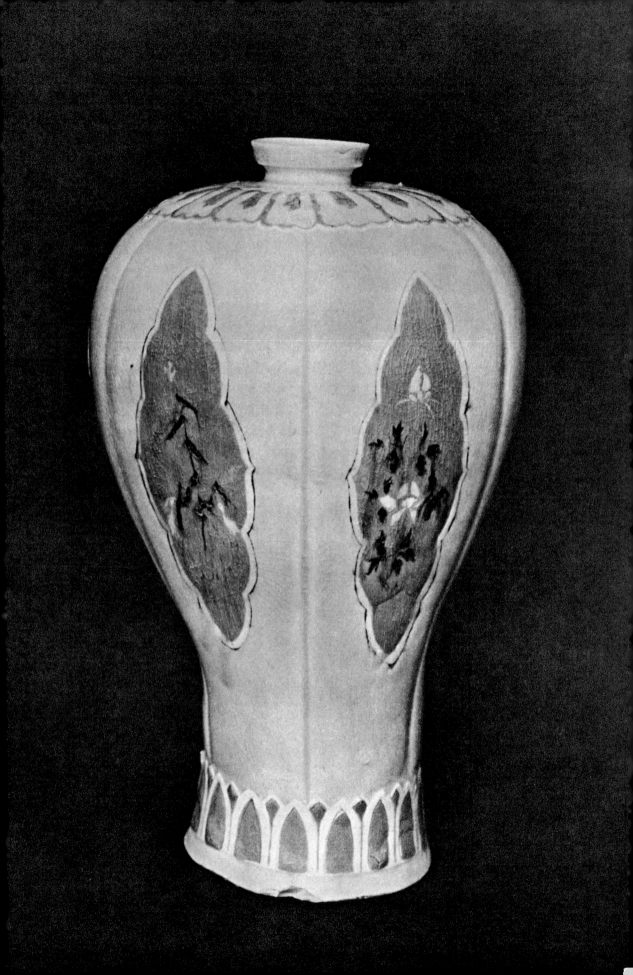

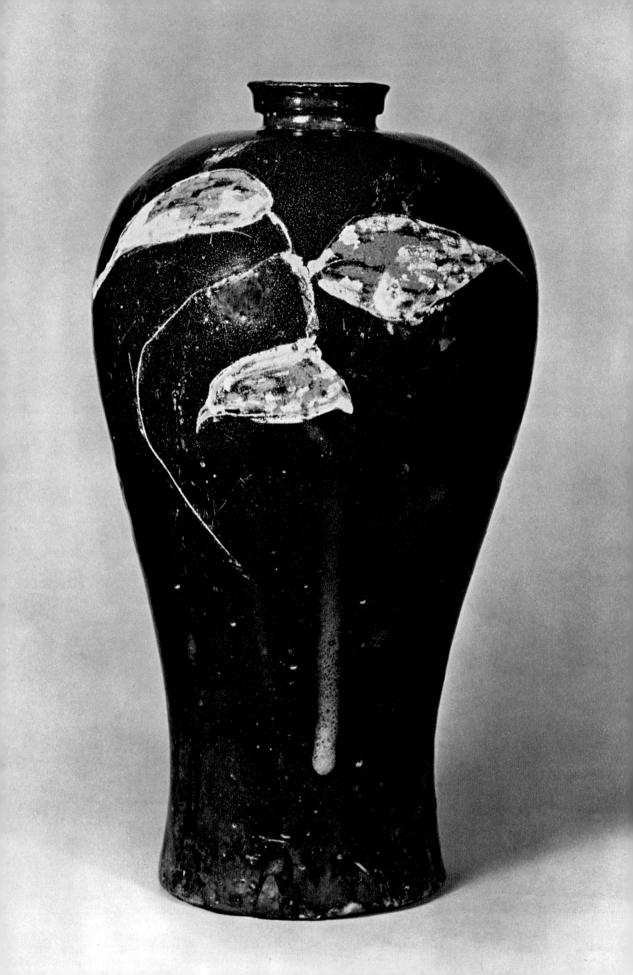

87 Apsara on the Temple Bell. Koryo
    Dynasty. Nagato-ichinomiya-jinja,
    Yamaguchi.

86 Vase with Ginseng-leaf Design in White,
    Black Ware. Koryo Dynasty.

88 Amulet Case. Silver. Koryo
Dynasty.

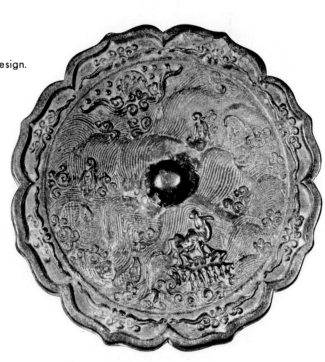

89 Box with Arabesque Design in Mother-of-pearl Inlay. Koryo Dynasty. National Museum, Tokyo.

90 Mirror with Sea-animal Design. Bronze. Koryo Dynasty.

91 Covered Box with Arabesque Design in Mother-of-pearl Inlay. Koryo Dynasty. Keishun-in, Kyoto.

92 Ewer with Inlaid Willow and Water-bird Design. Koryo
Dynasty. National Museum of Korea, Seoul.

93 Visit in Dream to T'ao-yüan (Detail). By An Kyon. Ink and
Faint Color on Silk. Yi Dynasty. Tenri Library, Tenri. Japan

94 Landscape and Flower-and-bird (Detail). Ink on
Paper. Yi Dynasty. Seiken-ji Temple, Shizuoka. Japan

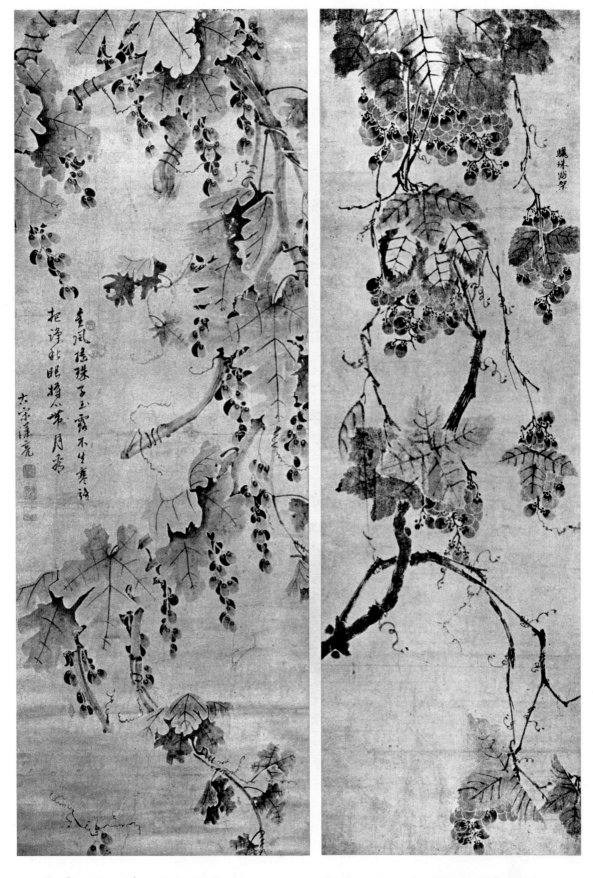

96 Grapevine. Ink on Paper. Yi Dynasty.　　　97 Grapevine. Ink on Paper. Yi Dynasty.

一覧無双

98 Grapevine and Squirrels. Ink on Paper.
    Yi Dynasty.

99   Myna Bird on Pine Branch. Ink on Paper.
      Yi Dynasty.

100 Wild-geese and Reeds. Ink on Silk.
      Yi Dynasty.

101 Bamboo and Rocks. Ink on Silk.
Yi Dynasty.

102 Autumn Landscape. Ink on Silk. Yi Dynasty.

103 Palsung-jon of Pobju-sa Temple. Wood.
Yi Dynasty. Poun-kun, Chungchong-pukdo.

104   Taesong-jon of the Confucian Temple Mun-myo.
Wood. Yi Dynasty. Seoul.

106 Flask with Arabesque Design, "Mishima" Type.
Yi Dynasty. From Cheju Island.

108 Tea Bowl, "Mishima" Type,
Incised Decoration. Yi Dynasty.

107 Jar with Fish and Bird Design, Painted
over Brush-mark Slip. Yi Dynasty.

109　Bowl with Brush-mark Slip and Scratch Design.
Yi Dynasty. Japan Folk Craft Museum, Tokyo.

110 Tea Bowl, "Mishima" Type with Brush-mark Slip.
Yi Dynasty. Japan Folk Craft Museum, Tokyo.

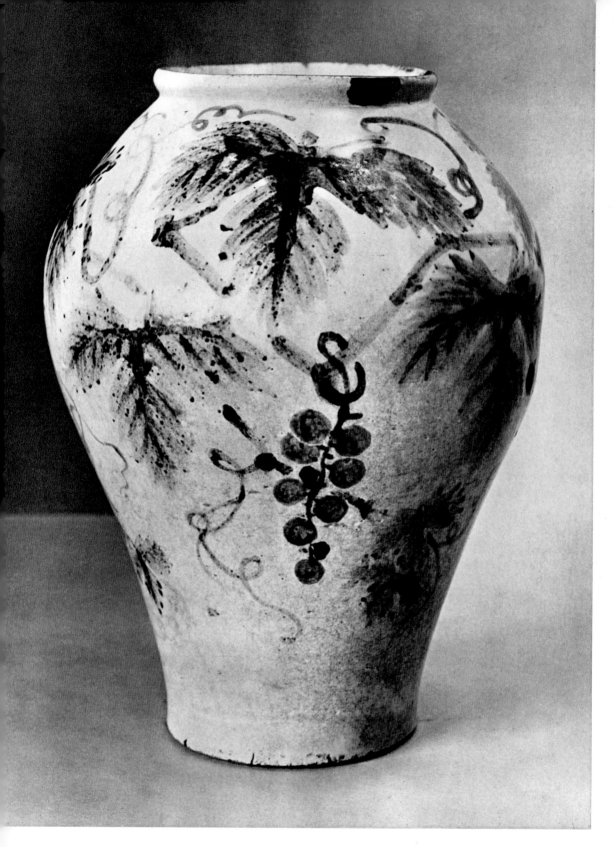

111 Jar with Grapevine Design, Underglaze Blue and Black-brown
Painting. Yi Dynasty. Japan Folk Craft Museum, Tokyo.

112 Tea Bowl with Black-brown Inlay Decoration.
Yi Dynasty. Japan Folk Craft Museum, Tokyo.

113 Jar with Heron Design, Underglaze
Black-brown. Yi Dynasty.

114   Jar with Grass Design, Underglaze
Black-brown. Yi Dynasty.

115 Jar with Dragon Design, Underglaze
Black-brown. Yi Dynasty.

116 Bowl with Water Fowl Design, Blue and White.
Yi Dynasty. Japan Folk Craft Museum, Tokyo.

117   Square Vase with Roundel Design,
      Blue and White. Yi Dynasty.

118 Flask with Pink-flower Design, Blue
and White. Yi Dynasty.

119   Ribbed Jar, White Porcelain. Yi Dynasty.

120　Vase, Underglaze Red. Yi Dynasty.

121 Octagonal Bottle, White Porcelain.
Yi Dynasty.

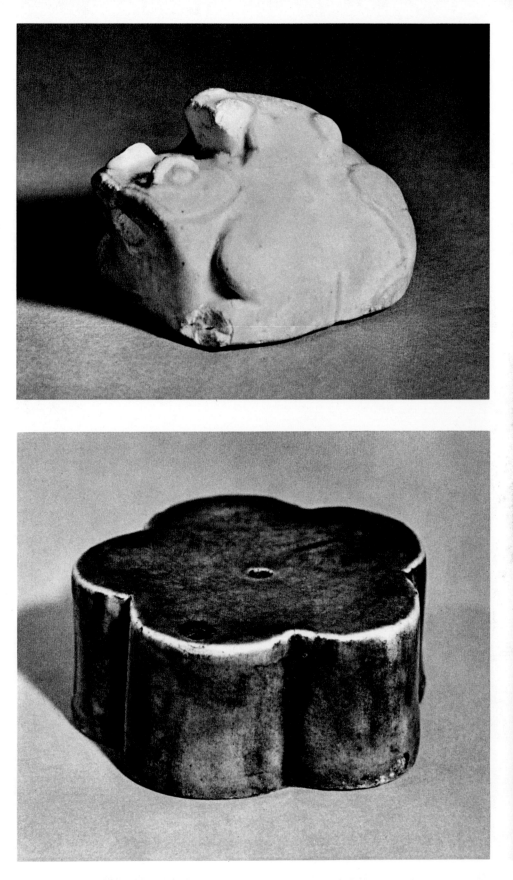

122 Water Dropper in Shape of Frog.
White Porcelain. Yi Dynasty.

123 Water Dropper in Shape of Plum
Blossom, Blue Glaze. Yi Dynasty.

124 Water Dropper in Shape of House,   125 Water Dropper with PlumBlossom Design,
     Blue and White. Yi Dynasty. Japan   Blue and White. Yi Dynasty.
     Folk Craft Museum, Tokyo.

126 Writing Box with Flower-and-bird Design in Mother-
of-pearl Inlay. Yi Dynasty. National Museum, Tokyo.

127 Box with Floral Patterns in Mother-of-pearl
Inlay. Yi Dynasty.

128 Box with Grapevine and Squirrel Design
in Mother-of-pearl Inlay. Yi Dynasty.

129   Seal Box. Wood. Yi Dynasty. Japan Folk Craft
Museum, Tokyo.